HARRAP'S

GERMAN
pocket
GRAMMAR

New York   Chicago   San Francisco   Lisbon   London   Madrid   Mexico City
Milan   New Delhi   San Juan   Seoul   Singapore   Sydney   Toronto

ISBN 978-0-07-163623-0
MHID 0-07-163623-4

McGraw-Hill books are available at special quantity discounts to use as
premiums and sales promotions or for use in corporate training programs.
To contact a representative, please visit the Contact Us pages at
www.mhprofessional.com.

Project Editors: Alex Hepworth, Kate Nicholson
With Helen Bleck

Designed by Chambers Harrap Publishers Ltd, Edinburgh
Typeset in Rotis Serif and Meta Plus by Macmillan Publishing Solutions

CONTENTS

INTRODUCTION

This German grammar from Chambers has been written to meet the needs of all students of German, and is particularly suited for those taking school examinations. The essential rules of the German language have been explained in terms that are as accessible as possible to all users. Where technical terms have been used then full explanations of these terms have also been supplied. There is also a full glossary of grammatical terminology on pages 7-14.

While literary aspects of the German language have not been ignored, the emphasis has been placed squarely on modern spoken German. This grammar, with its wealth of lively and typical illustrations of usage taken from the present-day language, is the ideal study aid for all levels – from the beginner who is starting to get to grips with the German language through to the advanced user who requires a comprehensive and readily accessible work of reference. All the changes due to the German spelling reforms have been integrated into the text.

For this new edition the text has been fully revised and updated, while the smart new two-colour design makes consultation even easier and more enjoyable.

Abbreviations used in the text:

acc	accusative
dat	dative
fem	feminine
gen	genitive
indef art	indefinite article
masc	masculine
neut	neuter
nom	nominative
pl	plural
pron	pronoun
sing	singular

1 GLOSSARY OF GRAMMATICAL TERMS

ABSTRACT An abstract noun is one which names a quality or a concept rather than a concrete physical object or a person. Examples of abstract nouns are **happiness, life, length**.

ACCUSATIVE The accusative is the case used when a noun or pronoun (and any related article and adjective) is the object of a verb. For example, in the phrases **I love him/this old city** the words **him** and **this old city** are objects and, in German, must be put in the accusative case. It is also used after certain prepositions, eg **für mich** (for me).

ACTIVE The active form of a verb is the basic form as in **I remember her**. It is normally opposed to the **PASSIVE** form of the verb as in **she will be remembered**.

ADJECTIVAL NOUN An adjectival noun is an adjective used as a noun. For example, the adjective **young** is used as a noun in **the young at heart**.

ADJECTIVE A describing word telling us what something or someone is like (eg **a small** house, the **Royal** Family, an **interesting** pastime).

ADVERB Adverbs are normally used with a verb to add extra information by indicating **how** the action is done (adverbs of manner), **when**, **where** and **with how much intensity** the action is done (adverbs of time, place and intensity), or **to what extent** the action is done (adverbs of quantity). Adverbs may also be used with an adjective or another adverb (eg **a very** attractive girl, **very** well).

AGREEMENT In German, words such as adjectives, articles and pronouns are said to agree in number, gender and case with the noun or pronoun they refer to. This means that their form changes according to the *number* of the noun (singular or plural), its *gender* (masculine, feminine or neuter) and its *case* (nominative, accusative, genitive or dative).

APPOSITION A word or phrase is said to be in apposition to another when it is placed directly after it without any joining word (eg Mr Jones, **our bank manager**, rang today).

ARTICLE *See* DEFINITE ARTICLE *and* INDEFINITE ARTICLE.

AUXILIARY Auxiliary verbs are used to form compound tenses of other verbs, eg *have* in I **have** seen or *will* in she **will** go. The main auxiliary verbs in German are sein, haben and werden.

CARDINAL Cardinal numbers are numbers such as one, two, ten, fourteen, as opposed to ORDINAL numbers (eg first, second).

CASE German has four cases (*see* NOMINATIVE, ACCUSATIVE, GENITIVE, DATIVE). Each case is indicated by the endings of nouns, adjectives and articles, and the forms or endings of pronouns.

CLAUSE A clause is a group of words which contains at least a subject and a verb: he said is a clause. A clause often contains more than this basic information, eg he said this to her yesterday. Sentences can be made up of several clauses, eg he said/he'd call me/if he were free. *See* SENTENCE.

COLLECTIVE A collective noun is one which names a group of people or things but which is singular in form. Examples of collective nouns are flock or fleet.

COLLOQUIAL Colloquial language is the sort of language that can be used in everyday informal conversation, but is avoided in formal writing such as business letters, legal documents *etc.*

COMPARATIVE The comparative forms of adjectives and adverbs are used to compare two things, persons or actions. In English, more ... than, -er than, less ... than and as ... as are used for comparison.

COMPLEMENT The complement is the part of the clause which completes the information on the subject. It may be a noun group (That is *a very difficult question,* She'll make *a good leader*), an adjective group (You seem *tired and stressed*) or a prepositional phrase, that is, a preposition plus a noun group (The cat is *in the garden*).

COMPOUND Compound tenses are verb tenses consisting of more than one element. In German, the compound tenses of a verb are formed by the AUXILIARY verb and the PAST PARTICIPLE and/or INFINITIVE: ich habe gesehen, er ist gekommen, er wird kommen.

COMPOUND NOUNS Compound nouns are nouns made up of two or more separate words. English examples are goalkeeper or dinner party. German compound nouns are normally written as a single word.

CONDITIONAL This mood is used to describe what someone would do, or something that would happen if a condition were fulfilled (eg I *would come* if I was well; the chair *would have broken* if he had sat on it).

CONJUGATION The conjugation of a verb is the set of different forms taken in the particular tenses and moods of that verb.

CONJUNCTION Conjunctions are linking words (eg and, but, or). They may be subordinating or coordinating. Coordinating conjunctions are words like und, aber, oder; subordinating conjunctions are words like weil, wenn, obgleich.

DATIVE The dative is the case used in German when a noun or pronoun (and any related article and adjective) is the indirect object of a verb. For example, in ich habe es ihm gegeben ('I gave it to him'), the word ihm is in the dative case. The dative is also used after certain prepositions, eg mit mir ('with me').

DECLENSION The declension of nouns and adjectives is the name given to the system of endings that they take.

DEFINITE ARTICLE The definite article is the in English and der, die, das in German.

DEMONSTRATIVE Demonstrative adjectives (eg this, that, these) and pronouns (eg this one, that one) are used to point out a particular person or thing.

DIRECT OBJECT This is a noun or a pronoun which in English follows a verb without any linking preposition, eg I met a *friend*. In German the direct object is always in the accusative case. (Note that in English a preposition is often omitted, eg I sent him a present: *him* is the equivalent of *to him*; *a present* is the direct object).

ENDING The ending of a verb is determined by the PERSON (1st/2nd/3rd) and NUMBER (singular/plural) of its subject. In German, nouns also have endings depending on their number and case.

EXCLAMATION. Words or phrases used to express surprise, annoyance *etc* (eg what!, wow!, how lucky!, what a nice day!).

FEMININE *See* GENDER

FINITE The finite verb is the form which has the endings indicating person and tense.

GENDER The gender of a noun indicates whether the noun is *masculine*, *feminine* or *neuter*. In German, the gender of a noun is not always determined by the sex of what it refers to, eg das Mädchen ('the girl') is a neuter noun.

GENITIVE The genitive case is used in German when some form of possession is being expressed, normally equivalent to the English use of the word of. For example, in the phrase the colour of the car, the words *of the car* must be in the genitive case in German.

IDIOM Idioms, or idiomatic expressions, are phrases which cannot normally be translated word for word. For example, it's raining cats and dogs is translated by es regnet Bindfäden.

IMPERATIVE A mood used for giving orders (eg stop!, don't go!) or for making suggestions (eg let's go).

INDEFINITE Indefinite pronouns are words that do not refer to a definite person or object (eg each, someone).

INDEFINITE ARTICLE The indefinite article is a in English and ein, eine, einen *etc* in German.

INDICATIVE The normal form of a verb as in I like, he came, we are trying. It used for asking questions and making statements, and is opposed to the subjunctive, conditional and imperative.

INDIRECT OBJECT This is a pronoun or noun which follows a verb sometimes with a linking preposition (usually to), eg I spoke to *my friend/him*, she gave *him* a kiss. In German the indirect object takes the dative case.

INFINITIVE The infinitive is the form of the verb as found in dictionaries. Thus to eat, to finish, to take are infinitives. In German, all infinitives end in -n: leben, gehen, lächeln, ärgern.

INTERROGATIVE Interrogative words are used to ask a QUESTION. This may be a direct question (*when* will you arrive?) or an indirect question (I don't know *when* he'll arrive).

MASCULINE *See* GENDER

MOOD The name given to the four main areas within which a verb is conjugated. *See* INDICATIVE, SUBJUNCTIVE, CONDITIONAL, IMPERATIVE.

NEUTER *See* GENDER

NOMINATIVE The nominative case is the case used when a noun or pronoun (and any related article and adjectives) is the subject of a verb, eg in the phrase the new caretaker speaks German, the words *the new caretaker* must be in the nominative case in German.

NOUN A naming word, which can refer to living creatures, things, people, places or abstract ideas, eg postman, cat, shop, Germany, life.

NUMBER The number of a noun indicates whether the noun is SINGULAR or PLURAL. A singular noun refers to one single thing or person (eg boy, train) and a plural noun to several (eg boys, trains).

OBJECT *See* DIRECT OBJECT, INDIRECT OBJECT

ORDINAL Ordinal numbers are first, second, third, fourth *etc*. In German, all ordinal numbers end in -te(r/s).

PASSIVE A verb is used in the passive when the subject of the verb does not perform the action but is subjected to it. In English, the passive is formed with a part of the verb to be and the past participle of the verb, eg he was rewarded. It is used in contrast to the ACTIVE.

PAST PARTICIPLE The past participle of a verb is the form which is used after **to have** in English to form the past tense, eg I have **eaten**, I have **said**, you have **tried**.

PERSON In any tense, there are three persons in the singular (1st: I ..., 2nd: you ..., 3rd: he/she/it ...), and three in the plural (1st: we ..., 2nd: you ..., 3rd: they ...). *See also* ENDING.

PERSONAL PRONOUNS Personal pronouns stand for a noun. In English they are words like **I, you, he/she/it, we, they** or **me, you, him/her/it, us, them**.

PLURAL *See* NUMBER

POSSESSIVE Possessives are used to indicate possession or ownership. They are words like **my/mine, your/yours, our/ours**.

PREPOSITION Prepositions are words such as **with, in, to, at**. They are normally followed by a noun or a pronoun.

PRESENT PARTICIPLE The present participle is the verb form which ends in **-ing** in English (**-end** in German).

PRONOUN A word which stands for a noun. The main categories of pronouns are:
* Personal pronouns (eg **you, him, us**)
* Possessive pronouns (eg **mine, yours, his**)
* Reflexive pronouns (eg **myself, himself**)
* Interrogative pronouns (eg **who?, what?, which?**)
* Relative pronouns (eg **who, which, that**)
* Demonstrative pronouns (eg **this, that, these**)
* Indefinite pronouns (eg **something, none**)

QUESTION There are two question forms: *direct* questions stand on their own and require a question mark at the end (eg *when* **will he come?**); *indirect* questions are introduced by a clause and require no question mark (eg *I wonder* **when he will come**).

REFLEXIVE Reflexive verbs 'reflect' the action back onto the subject (eg I dressed *myself*). They are always found with a reflexive pronoun and are much more common in German than in English.

SENTENCE A sentence is a group of words made up of one or more clauses (*see* CLAUSE). The end of a sentence is indicated by a punctuation mark (usually a full stop, a question mark or an exclamation mark).

SINGULAR *See* NUMBER

STEM *See* VERB STEM

SUBJECT The subject of a verb is the noun or pronoun which performs the action. In the sentences *the train left early* and *she bought a record, the train* and *she* are the subjects.

SUBJUNCTIVE The subjunctive is a verb form used to express wishes, doubts and possibilities which is rarely used in English (eg if I *were* you, God *save* the Queen). It is more common in German.

SUPERLATIVE The form of an adjective or an adverb which, in English, is marked by the most ..., the -est or the least ....

TENSE Verbs are used in tenses, which indicate when an action takes place, eg in the present, the past, the future.

VERB A 'doing' word, which usually describes an action (eg to sing, to work, to watch). Some verbs describe a state (eg to be, to have, to hope).

VERB STEM The stem of a verb is its 'basic unit' to which the various endings are added. To find the stem of a German verb remove -en or -n from the infinitive. The stem of sagen is sag, the stem of ärgern is ärger.

VOICE The two voices of a verb are its ACTIVE and PASSIVE forms.

2 ARTICLES

The form of any article depends on whether the noun following it is masculine, feminine or neuter, whether it is singular or plural and which case it is in.

 A THE DEFINITE ARTICLE

1 Forms

a) The definite article in English has only one form – 'the'.

The definite article in German changes its ending according to the gender and case of the noun, and whether it is singular or plural. For the use of the cases, *see* pp 51-3.

	MASCULINE	FEMININE	NEUTER	PLURAL ALL GENDERS
nom	der	die	das	die
acc	den	die	das	die
gen	des	der	des	der
dat	dem	der	dem	den

die Lehrerin kommt später
the teacher's coming later

kennst du den Sänger?
do you know the singer?

der Anfang des Liedes
the beginning of the song

hier sind die Äpfel
here are the apples

es steht auf dem Tisch
it's on the table

sag es den anderen!
tell it to the others

b) *combined with prepositions*

Some articles can be combined with a preceding preposition, for example an + das becomes ans. In some cases these combined

forms are normal in both spoken and written German, in others
the combined form is only used in spoken German:

das	ans, ins
	spoken German only: aufs, durchs, fürs, hinters, übers, ums, unters, vors
	sie ging ans Fenster
	she went to the window
	es geht ums Überleben
	it's a question of survival
dem	am, beim, im, vom, zum
	spoken German only: hinterm, überm, unterm, vorm
	ich gehe zum Bäcker
	I'm going to the baker's
	vorm Haus steht ein Baum
	there's a tree in front of the house
der	zur
	er fuhr zur Erholung in den Schwarzwald
	he went to the Black Forest on a health cure

The combined forms are sometimes not used if the writer or
speaker wishes to emphasise the article:

wo? – ach, in *dem* Wirtshaus
where? – oh, in *that* pub

The combined forms are not normally used if the noun is
followed by a relative clause (*see* pp 103-07):

in dem Café, das gestern eröffnet wurde
in the café that opened yesterday

2 Use

As in English, the definite article is used to indicate a specific
person or thing:

der Zirkus kommt
the circus is coming

die Disco hinter dem Rathaus
the disco behind the town hall

Apart from cases where the usage is similar to English, the definite article is used:

a) *with the names of certain countries and geographical regions, especially ones that are feminine:*

die Slowakei	**die Türkei**	**die Schweiz**
Slovakia	Turkey	Switzerland
das Elsass	**der Sudan**	**der Balkan**
Alsace	the Sudan	the Balkans
in der Türkei	**wir fahren in die Schweiz**	
in Turkey	we're going to Switzerland	

With some countries the article is optional:

(der) Iran	**(der) Irak**	**(der) Libanon**
Iran	Iraq	Lebanon

im/in Iran
in Iran

Note that all geographical names have a definite article if they are preceded by an adjective:

das alte Berlin
old Berlin

except for the adjectives ganz and halb:

ganz/das ganze Schottland	**halb/das halbe Europa**
the whole of Scotland	half of Europe

b) *generally with abstract nouns:*

für die Freiheit kämpfen
to fight for freedom

nichts geht über die Gesundheit
nothing is more important than health

c) *with activities such as the arts, business, science, sports:*

eine Sendung über die Botanik
a programme about botany

eine Einführung in das Bankwesen
an introduction to banking

die Entwicklung der Chemie   **die moderne Leichtathletik**
the development of chemistry   modern athletics

Note that there is no article when such words are used for school/university subjects:

wir haben heute Chemie   **Turnen ist mein Lieblingsfach**
we have chemistry today   P.E. is my favourite subject

d) *with Mensch when it refers to the species:*

der Mensch ist ein Gewohnheitstier
man is a creature of habit

e) *with the seasons, months, meals and times of the day:*

am Abend	**im Mai**	**zum Abendessen**
in the evening	in May	for dinner
der Frühling kommt	**in der Dämmerung**	
spring is coming	at twilight	

Note

- the article is not used when such words are combined with adjectives to form adverb phrases. *Compare:*

im Mai
next May

and

wir ziehen nächsten Mai um
we're moving in May

- the article is not used after es ist/wird

es ist schon Tag   **es wird bald Winter**
it's day already   it'll soon be winter

f) *as an alternative to* pro *to translate 'per':*

150 Kilometer pro/die Stunde
150 kilometres per hour

g) *with parts of the body and clothes where English would use the possessive:*

heb die Hand!   **zieh ihm die Jacke aus!**
raise your hand!   take his jacket off

die Frau mit dem roten Haar
the woman with red hair

h) *with types of transport, especially after prepositions:*

mit dem Wagen   **mit dem Rad**   **auf dem Schiff**
by car   by bicycle   on board ship

> Note
>
> In many expressions composed of verb + preposition + noun the article used does not correspond to the English equivalent:
>
> **zum Stehen kommen**   **jemanden zur Vernunft bringen**
> to come to a halt   to make someone see reason
> **aus der Mode sein**
> to be out of fashion
>
> Such expressions must be learnt as a whole.

3 The definite article used as a pronoun

a) The definite article can be used as an alternative to the personal pronoun (*see* pp 87-91); this usage is most common in spoken German and usually occurs when the pronoun occupies the first position in the sentence:

Paul Gruber? der ist mein Freund
Paul Gruber? he's my friend

Paul Gruber? den kenn' ich nicht
Paul Gruber? I don't know him

b) The neuter article, **das**, is used as a demonstrative (translated by the English 'that') to refer back to people, things and whole sentences:

die Frau? das ist meine Mutter
that woman? that's my mother

beeil dich! das ist der Zug
hurry up, that's the train

du fährst mit? das ist vernünftig
you're coming? that's sensible

c) The definite article is used with the relative pronoun for the English construction 'the one/the person who':

der, der es getan hat, soll sich melden
the one who did it should own up

gib es dem, der es am meisten braucht
give it to the one who needs it most

d) When used as a pronoun, the definite article has separate genitive forms:

MASCULINE	FEMININE	NEUTER	PLURAL ALL GENDERS
dessen	deren	dessen	derer

These forms are relatively uncommon. They are used in sentences of the type in (c) above:

auf Kosten derer, die arbeitslos sind
at the expense of those out of work

e) The genitive forms above are also used as an alternative to the possessives (**mein**=my *etc*) when the possessive itself might be ambiguous. The only difference is that the plural form is **deren** in these cases. This happens where there are two people to whom the possessive might refer back. Thus in the sentence

'she saw Fiona and her husband'

it is not clear whether it is Fiona's or the subject's husband that is being referred to. The dessen forms refer back to the last mentioned person. So, in:

sie sah Petra und ihren Mann

it is unclear whether she saw Petra's or her own husband, but in:

sie sah Petra und deren Mann

it is clear that she saw Petra and her – Petra's – husband.

 B THE INDEFINITE ARTICLE

1 Forms

The indefinite article in English has only one form: 'a' (or 'an').

In German the indefinite article changes its ending according to the gender and case of the noun after it. *For the use of the cases see* **pp 51-3**.

	MASCULINE	FEMININE	NEUTER
nom	ein	eine	ein
acc	einen	eine	ein
gen	eines	einer	eines
dat	einem	einer	einem

eine Frau
a woman

hier ist ein Stuhl
here is a chair

nimm einen Stuhl!
take a chair

die Mutter einer Schülerin
the mother of a schoolgirl

mit einem schweren Hammer
with a heavy hammer

2 Use

a) As in English, the indefinite article is used with nouns to indicate someone or something which is not precisely specified:

hast du eine Zeitung gesehen?
have you seen a newspaper?

ich möchte ein Bier
I would like a beer

b) Unlike English, German omits the indefinite article

(i) before the names of occupations or similar functions when they have no adjective:

ich möchte Bäcker werden
I would like to be a baker

er ist Vegetarier
he is a vegetarian

sie ist Katholikin geworden
she has become a Catholic

but: **sie ist eine bekannte Pilotin**
she is a famous pilot

(ii) after als = as:

ich komme als Freund
I come as a friend

sie gilt als ausgezeichnete Ärztin
she is considered an excellent doctor

(iii) with names of nationalities used after the verb 'to be':

er ist Deutscher
he is a German

sie ist Französin von Geburt
she is a Frenchwoman by birth

3 The indefinite article used as a pronoun

a) *special forms*

When the indefinite article is used by itself as a pronoun, it has the same forms as above, except that the masculine nominative is einer and the neuter nominative and accusative is ein(e)s.

b) *use*

Used as a pronoun, it refers to some unspecified person or thing:

ein(e)s von den Mädchen
one of the girls

einer meiner Freunde
one of my friends

It is often an alternative to man:

was soll einer da machen?
what should one do?

> ## Note
>
> The accusative and dative forms are used for the accusative and
> dative of man:
>
> **man soll es offen sagen, wenn einem etwas nicht gefällt**
> you should say so openly if you don't like something
>
> **es kann einen schon ärgern, wenn man ...**
> it can be very annoying if one ...

4 irgendein

irgendein is usually translated by 'some ... or other'. It has the same
endings as ein and can be used both as an article and as a pronoun:

irgendeiner hat's gesagt
someone or other said it

irgendeine Ausrede
any old excuse

wir werden irgendeinen Film sehen
we'll see some film or other

For the plural, irgendwelche is used:

hat jemand irgendwelche Fragen?
has anyone any questions at all?

5 The indefinite article as adjective

ein can be used as an adjective after the definite article, a
demonstrative or possessive. In such cases it has the appropriate
adjective endings (*see* pp 64-72):

der eine Besucher bleibt länger
one of the visitors is staying longer

die Frau des einen lebt noch
the wife of one of them is still alive

 C kein (NO, NOT A, NOT ANY)

kein has the same endings as the indefinite article ein, but also has
a plural form:

	MASCULINE	FEMININE	NEUTER	PLURAL ALL GENDERS
nom	kein	keine	kein	keine
acc	keinen	keine	kein	keine
gen	keines	keiner	keines	keiner
dat	keinem	keiner	keinem	keinen

a) It is used as a negative both for the indefinite article and for
   words without an article:

   positive

   ich habe Zeit
   I have time

   ich habe einen Computer
   I have a computer

   ich habe Ferien
   I'm on holiday

   negative

   sie hat keine Zeit
   she has no time

   er hat keinen Computer
   he hasn't got a computer

   er hat keine Ferien
   he's not on holiday

   It is always used in cases where English uses 'not a':

   kein einziger Mensch kam
   not a single person came

b) kein can also be used by itself, as a pronoun.

   In that case, the masculine nominative singular is keiner, the
   neuter singular nominative and accusative is kein(e)s:

   keiner weiß, wo er steckt
   no-one knows where he is

D **derjenige AND derselbe**
(THE ONE; THE SAME)

These are declined in two parts, the der part having the forms of
the definite article, the second part having regular endings for an
adjective after the definite article (*see* pp 64-6):

	MASCULINE	**FEMININE**	**NEUTER**	**PLURAL ALL GENDERS**
nom	derjenige	diejenige	dasjenige	diejenigen
acc	denjenigen	diejenige	dasjenige	diejenigen
gen	desjenigen	derjenigen	desjenigen	derjenigen
dat	demjenigen	derjenigen	demjenigen	denjenigen

derselbe follows the same pattern.

a) derjenige can be used before a noun or by itself, as a pronoun.
It is used to specify someone or something about which more
precise information is going to be given. Thus it is always
followed either by a relative clause or by a noun in the genitive
or by a preposition + noun.

A noun preceded by derjenige is always followed by a relative
clause. derjenige tends to be avoided, especially in colloquial
German.

diejenigen, die schon Karten haben, sollen vortreten
those who already have tickets should come forward

kennst du diejenigen Mitglieder, die dagegen gestimmt haben?
do you know the members who voted against?

b) derselbe is used both before a noun and by itself, as a pronoun.
It is the equivalent to the English 'the same', except that it is
written as one word:

das ist nicht mehr dieselbe Mannschaft
they're not the same team any more

es läuft auf dasselbe hinaus
it amounts to the same thing

> ### Note
>
> The article (der etc) in derselbe can combine with some
> prepositions. It is then written as two words:
>
> **im selben Haus**   **zur selben Schule**
> in the same house   to the same school
>
> **ins selbe Theater**
> to the same theatre

c) **dergleichen** *('suchlike, of that kind')*

der gleiche is written as two words, except for **dergleichen**
meaning 'suchlike'. **dergleichen** can be used before nouns or by
itself, but in either case it does not change its form:

dergleichen Fälle   **nichts dergleichen**
cases like this   nothing of the sort

E DEMONSTRATIVES

dieser	jener	jeder	mancher	solcher	aller	welcher
this	that	each, every	some, many a	such	all	which

These are generally called demonstrative adjectives (or pronouns).
Adjectives that follow them have the same endings as after the
definite article.

1 Forms

	MASCULINE	FEMININE	NEUTER	PLURAL ALL GENDERS
nom	dieser	diese	dieses	diese
acc	diesen	diese	dieses	diese
gen	dieses	dieser	dieses	dieser
dat	diesem	dieser	diesem	diesen

The others have the same endings, except that jeder only occurs in the singular.

2 Use

a) dieser *('this')*

Note that the neuter nominative and accusative is sometimes shortened to dies. dieser is used to point to a person or thing. It can be used before a noun or by itself, as a pronoun. It is very close to the English 'this':

gefällt dir dieser Mantel?
do you like this coat?

nein, ich nehme diesen
no, I'll take this one

It is often emphasised by the addition of hier or da after it or after the noun it goes with:

diese Jacke hier ist schöner
this jacket here is nicer

aber probier diese da an
but try on that one there

When standing alone before the verb sein (in all tenses) it is usually in the dies form, whatever the number or gender of the words it refers back to; the verb is singular or plural, according to the number of the noun following:

dies sind meine Eltern
these are my parents

dies hier ist meine Tochter
this is my daughter here

dies(es) waren die besten Bilder
these were the best pictures

b) jener *('that')*

jener is relatively little used in colloquial German. The word for 'that' as opposed to 'this' is usually der/die/das (*see* c) below). In the following, somewhat formal, sentence, jene could be replaced by die, but is slightly more emphatic:

er zeigte jene Kraft, die ihm zu vielen Siegen verholfen hatte
he showed that strength which had brought him many victories

jener and dieser are used for 'the former' and 'the latter':

Männer und Frauen, diese sorgen für andere, jene für sich
men and women, the former care for themselves, the latter for others

c) **der, die, das**

The definite article is also used in German to mean 'that'. Sometimes the word **da** is also added after the noun:

der Mann (da)   **die Schule (da)**
that man   that school

d) **jeder** *('each, every')*

jeder can be used before the noun or by itself, as a pronoun:

jedes Kind weiß das   **jeder soll kommen**
every child knows that   everyone's to come

The term **jedermann** is felt to be slightly stilted; **jeder** is the usual German for 'everyone'.

jeder can be emphasised by the addition of **ein** before it; it still has the same endings:

ein jeder muss was mitbringen
everyone has to bring something

e) **mancher** *('some, many a')*

mancher can be used before the noun or by itself, as a pronoun. It indicates an uncertain number and translation can range from 'a few' to 'some', even 'many':

manche älteren Leute   **manche hundert Euro**
some older people   a few hundred euros

mancher Mann möchte reich sein   **manches blieb unerledigt**
many a man would like to be rich   quite a lot of things were unfinished

i) In the singular **manch** can be used without endings before an adjective + noun:

sie hat manch schöne Stadt gesehen
she has seen many a fair city

This usage is highly literary.

    ii) **manch** without endings can also be used before the indefinite article:

    manch eine interessante Geschichte   **manch ein Roman**
    many an interesting story   many a novel

    Used without a noun the masculine nominative is **manch einer**:

    manch einer erfährt das zu spät
    many a man learns that too late

f) solcher ('such, such a')

    i) In the singular **solcher** is rarely used with particular persons or objects. It is normally used with names of qualities, abstract nouns or substances.

    solches Wetter!   **mit solcher Geschwindigkeit, dass ...**
    such weather   with such speed that ...

    With particular persons or objects it is common to use **so ein**:

    so ein Fahrer   **haben Sie so eine Schüssel?**
    a driver like that   do you have a bowl like this?

    ii) In the plural it can be used with all nouns:

    solche Frauen sind gefährlich
    such women are dangerous

    iii) It can also be used by itself, as a pronoun, usually in the plural:

    ich kenne auch solche
    I know people/things like that, too

    In the singular it is only commonly used without a noun when it is neuter, in the form **solches**:

    hast du je solches gehört?
    have you ever heard anything like it?

    iv) **solch** can be used without endings before an adjective + noun:

    ein solch altes Schloss   **solch schicke Möbel**
    such an old castle   such smart furniture

v) solch without endings can also be used with the indefinite article:

solch ein altes Schloss　　**mit solch einem Freund**
such an old castle　　with such a friend

Used without a noun the masculine nominative is solch einer, the neuter nominative and accusative solch eines:

solch einer war's　　**hast du je solch einen gesehen?**
it was one like that　　have you ever seen one like him?

vi) solcher can also be used after ein or kein. In that case it has the normal adjective endings (*see* pp **67-8**).

Compare:
bei solchem schrecklichem Sturm
during such a terrible storm
with:
bei einem solchen schrecklichen Sturm

g) aller *('all, all the')*

i) In the singular aller can only be used together with nouns denoting qualities or substances or abstract nouns:

bei aller Bewunderung　　**er hat alles Geld ausgegeben**
in spite of all my admiration　　he spent all the money

In the plural it can be used before any noun:

alle Spieler　　**für alle Kunden**
all players　　for all customers

die beste von allen Gruppen
the best of all groups

In the neuter singular and in the plural it can be used by itself, as a pronoun:

alles in Ordnung?　　**nach allem, was du mir gesagt hast**
everything all right?　　after all you've told me

Sie müssen alle kommen　　**alle waren dagegen**
you must all come　　everyone was against it

Note

- Note the common expressions:

alle Welt   **die ganze Welt**
everybody   the whole world

- with most masculine and neuter nouns in the genitive singular
the normal form is allen:

allen Ernstes
in all seriousness

ii) Before an article, demonstrative or possessive the normal
form is all, without any ending; the article, demonstrative or
possessive retains its normal endings.

Note that there is no German equivalent to 'of' in the English
'all of':

all unsere Bekannten
all of our acquaintances, everyone we know

mit all diesem Geld   **all die Männer**
with all this money   all of the men

As an alternative to all das and all dies, das alles and dies alles
are possible.

Word order: after a pronoun:

es alles   **mit uns allen**   **für sie alle**
all of it   with all of us   for all of them

but:
before beide or a number:

alle beide   **von allen vier(en)**
both of them   of all four of them

There are two possible orders for this; 'all three came' can be
translated by:

alle drei sind gekommen
or
sie sind alle drei gekommen

h) **welcher?** *('which?')*

i) **welcher** is the interrogative article (sometimes called the interrogative adjective or pronoun). It can be used both before nouns and by itself, as a pronoun.

welche Farbe nehmen wir?
which colour shall we choose?

bei welcher Familie wohnt sie?
which family does she live with?

welches gefällt dir am besten?
which one do you like best?

welche kommen mit?
which of them are coming with us?

ii) Before the verb 'to be' (in any tense) the form **welches** is often used for all genders, singular and plural. The verb is singular or plural according to the number of the noun following:

welches ist der nächste Weg?
which is the shortest way?

welches (welche) waren die besten?
which were the best?

iii) **welch** may be used without endings before an adjective + noun to express an exclamation. This usage is rather literary, **was für ein** being generally preferred in colloquial German:

welch furchtbarer Kampf!
what a fearsome battle!

was für ein schlechtes Spiel!
what a poor game!

iv) **welch** can be used with the indefinite article before a noun to express an exclamation:

welch ein schrecklicher Kerl!
what an awful bloke!

v) **welcher** can also be used before a noun for exclamations; it is felt to be very stilted, although some standard phrases with feminine nouns are less so:

welche Freude!
what joy!

welche Ehre!
what an honour!

welche Schande!
what a disgrace!

vi) As an interrogative, **welcher** can introduce a clause which is the object of a verb of telling, showing *etc*; the verb in the **welcher** clause then goes to the end. **welcher** can be used in this way either before a noun or alone:

sag mir, welche CD mehr kostet
tell me which CD costs more

weißt du, welche mehr kostet?
do you know which one costs more?

vii) welcher can be used alone as an indefinite pronoun, replacing *etwas, einige etc.* In this usage it does not indicate a question. This is a very common colloquial usage:

ich hab kein Geld mehr. Hast du welches?
I've no money left. Have you any?

lass sie zu Hause, ich habe welche
leave them at home, I've got some

Note that the negative of welcher in this use is kein:

bring sie mit, ich hab keine
bring them with you, I haven't any

viii) welcher can be used as a relative pronoun without indicating a question. It is less common than der/die/das but is useful to avoid repetition:

das ist die Bluse, welche sie gewählt hat
that's the blouse she chose

wähle die, welche dir gefallen
choose the ones that you like

 THE POSSESSIVE

1 Forms

There is a possessive form for each of the personal pronouns:

PRONOUN	POSSESSIVE
ich	mein
du	dein
er	sein

sie	ihr
es	sein
wir	unser
ihr	euer
Sie	Ihr
sie	ihr

They have the same endings as ein and kein, depending on the gender, number and case of the noun following:

	MASCULINE	**FEMININE**	**NEUTER**	**PLURAL**
nom	mein	meine	mein	meine
acc	meinen	meine	mein	meine
gen	meines	meiner	meines	meiner
dat	meinem	meiner	meinem	meinen

with the same endings for dein, sein *etc*:

deine Tasche	**mit unserer Hilfe**	**für Ihre Kinder**
your bag	with our help	for your children

Note

- euer generally drops the -e- if it has an ending: eure, euren *etc*; unser often drops the -e- in spoken German, but it is normally kept when written.

- The possessives keep the same endings when they are preceded by aller, dieser, jener:

  mit aller seiner Geschicklichkeit   **diese meine Freunde**
  with all his skill   my friends here

  but: **diese alten Freunde von mir**
          these old friends of mine

- For the replacement of the possessive by dessen or deren, *see* pp 20-1.

2 Use

a) The possessive can also be used by itself, as a pronoun; in such cases the masculine nominative has the form meiner, deiner, seiner *etc*, and the neuter nominative and accusative have the form meines, deines, seines *etc*. Colloquially meines *etc* is often shortened to meins *etc*:

leih mir dein Rad, mein(e)s ist kaputt
lend me your bike, mine is broken

das ist ihr Platz, und das ist seiner
that's her place and that's his

b) As an adjectival noun the possessive has some idiomatic usages:

die Seinen his family	**sie hat das Ihre getan** she did her bit
grüß die Deinen best wishes to your family	

In sentences with noun + sein ('to be') + possessive, the possessives (except Ihr/ihr) often have no ending whatever the gender or number:

der Pulli ist mein that sweater is mine	**der Sieg war unser** victory was ours

c) The possessive can be used with the definite article as a pronoun (alternative to a) above). In such cases it has the endings of an adjective after the definite article. This usage is generally regarded as literary:

dieser Bleistift ist der meine
this pencil is mine

du hast kein Auto? fahr mit dem meinen
you've no car? take mine

d) A further alternative is to use the form of the possessive plus -ig with the definite article: der meinige, der deinige, der seinige, der ihrige, der unsrige, der eurige, der Ihrige, der ihrige. This usage is also regarded as rather literary.

3 NOUNS

Nouns are naming words, which refer to persons, animals, things or abstract ideas. In German all nouns, not just proper names, are written beginning with a capital letter:

Haus
house

Ball
ball

A GENDER

German nouns are either masculine, feminine or neuter in gender. The nouns themselves normally do not show this, but any preceding adjective or article 'agrees' with the noun by having the appropriate ending showing its gender plus number and case.

The gender should be learnt along with the noun, but often the meaning or ending will help you determine it, as set out in the guidelines below.

1 Masculine

a) *by meaning*

    i) names of male humans and animals:

        der Sohn   **der Student**   **der Hahn**
        son   student   cock

        The name for the species may be masculine, feminine or neuter:

        der Elefant   **die Schlange**   **das Kamel**
        elephant   snake   camel

    ii) names of days, months, seasons:

        nächsten Mittwoch   **letzten Mai**   **der Herbst**
        next Wednesday   last May   autumn

iii) points of the compass, winds, *etc*:

der Süden	der Monsun	der Hagel
south	monsoon	hail

iv) makes of cars:

ein BMW	ein Opel	ein Cadillac

but:

motorcycles are feminine:

die BMW	die Harley-Davidson

v) names of rock and soil types:

der Quarz	der Basalt	der Lehm
quartz	basalt	clay

but: die Kreide
chalk

b) *by ending*

-en	der Hafen	der Wagen
	harbour	car
-er	der Arbeiter	der Kopfhörer
	worker	headphones
but:	das Fenster	das Messer
	window	knife
	die Mutter	die Tochter
	mother	daughter

and a few other neuter and feminine nouns

-ich	der Teppich	der Gänserich
	carpet	gander
-ig	der König	
	king	
-ismus	der Terrorismus	
	terrorism	
-ist	der Optimist	
	optimist	
-ling	der Frühling	mein Liebling
	spring	my darling

-or	**der Horror**	**der Motor**
	horror	motor
consonant + s	**der Schnaps**	**der Lachs**
	schnapps	salmon

2 Feminine

a) *by meaning*

    i) names for female humans and animals:

| **die Mutter** | **meine Frau** | **eine Kuh** |
| the mother | my wife | a cow |

    ii) names for female occupations derived by adding -in to the masculine:

| **die Ärztin** | **die Journalistin** | **die Geologin** |
| doctor | journalist | geologist |

> ### Note
>
> Names of chemicals ending in -in are neuter:
>
> **das Benzin**
> petrol

    iii) names of most common trees, fruits and flowers:

	die Pappel	**die Kirsche**	**die Ananas**
	poplar	cherry	pineapple
	die Kiefer	**die Nelke**	**die Rose**
	pine	carnation	rose
but:	**der Ahorn**	**der Apfel**	**der Pfirsich**
	maple	apple	peach

    iv) makes of aeroplane and names of ships:

| | **die Boeing** | **die Graf Spee** |
| *but:* | **der Starfighter** | **der Airbus** |

    v) numbers:

| **eine Null** | **die Sieben** |
| zero | (number) seven |

b) *by ending*

-a	**die Kamera**	**die Tuba**
	camera	tuba
-ei	**die Kartei**	
	card index	

but: not compounds of **das Ei** (egg)

-enz	**die Frequenz**	
	frequency	
-heit	**die Freiheit**	
	freedom	
-ie	**die Chemie**	
	chemistry	
but:	**das Genie**	
	genius	
-ik	**die Technik**	
	technology	
but:	**der Atlantik**	**der Pazifik**
	Atlantic	Pacific
	der Katholik	
	Catholic	
-keit	**die Süßigkeit**	
	sweet	
-schaft	**die Mannschaft**	
	team	
-ung	**die Eroberung**	
	conquest	
but:	**der Schwung**	
	verve	
-tät	**die Pubertät**	
	puberty	
-tion	**die Reaktion**	
	reaction	
-ur	**die Natur**	
	nature	

3 Neuter

a) *by meaning*

i) names for the young of humans and animals:

das Kind   **das Baby**
child   baby

das Junge des Elefanten
the elephant calf

Note that **das Junge** is an adjectival noun; *for endings see*
section 4 *below.*

das Kalb   **das Lamm**   **das Fohlen**
calf   lamb   foal

ii) names of continents, towns and most countries:

das Europa der 20er-Jahre   **das Berlin meiner Kindheit**
the Europe of the twenties   the Berlin of my childhood

das heutige Deutschland
modern-day Germany

but: names of countries always preceded by the definite article are
usually feminine or plural:

die Schweiz   **die Türkei**   **die USA**
Switzerland   Turkey   the USA

iii) most names for metals, chemical elements and drugs:

das Messing   **das Uran**   **das Aspirin**
brass   uranium   aspirin

b) *by form*

i) nouns formed from other parts of speech, especially infinitives:

das Vergnügen   **sein Ja geben**   **das Hin und Her**
pleasure   to say yes   long deliberation

ii) diminutives with the endings -chen, -lein:

das Mädchen   **das Fräulein**   **das Städtchen**
girl   young woman   small town

iii) fractions (which take the suffix -tel):

ein Sechstel
a sixth

iv) collectives beginning with the prefix **Ge-**:

das Gebirge   **das Gerede**
the mountains   talk, gossip

c) *by ending*

-ing	**das Hearing**	**das Meeting**
-ma	**das Thema**	**das Dogma**
	subject	dogma
-ment	**das Regiment**	**das Appartement**
	regiment	flat
but:	**der Zement**	
	cement	
-tum	**das Eigentum**	
	property	
but:	**der Irrtum**	**der Reichtum**
	mistake	wealth
-um	**das Zentrum**	
	centre	

4 Adjectival nouns

All adjectives – and many past participles – can be made into nouns. As nouns, they begin with a capital letter but they keep the adjective endings:

der Deutsche	*but*	**ein Deutscher**
the German		a German
viele Deutsche	*but*	**alle Deutschen**
many Germans		all Germans

For the full list of endings see **pp 64–72.**

a) *masculine and feminine*

Masculine and feminine nouns formed from adjectives generally refer to people:

der Erste	**die Letzte**	**ein Neuer**
the first one	the last one	a new one

> ## Note
>
> When an adjective refers back to a noun there is no capital letter, the noun previously mentioned being understood:
>
> **zwei Läufer kommen, der deutsche führt knapp**
> there are two runners coming, the German is just in the lead
>
> *but*
>
> **der Deutsche hat gewonnen**
> the German won

b) *neuter*

Neuter nouns formed from adjectives most commonly refer to abstract ideas or qualities indicated by the adjective:

das Beste	**das Erschreckende**
the best	what is frightening

das eben Gesagte
what has just been said

   i) Such nouns are often used with an + dative:

     das Interessante an dieser Geschichte
     what is interesting about this story

     das Schlimmste an der Sache
     the worst thing about it

   ii) Such nouns are often used after etwas, nichts, viel, wenig, alles:

etwas Leckeres	**nichts Neues**	**alles Gute**
something tasty	nothing new	all the best

c) *names of colours*

Names for colours are formed from the adjective but there are forms both with and without the adjective ending.

   i) The form without the adjective ending is usually the name for the general colour:

   das Blau des Himmels
   the blue of the sky

   Rot steht dir nicht
   red doesn't suit you

   ii) The form with the adjective ending usually refers to some specific item of that colour:

   das Weiße seiner Augen
   the whites of his eyes

   das Gelbe vom Ei
   the yellow of the egg

Note

- For traffic lights the forms are Rot and Grün:

  bei Rot soll man halten, bei Grün darf man fahren
  you should stop on red, but at the green light you can go

- Note the plural for various shades of the same colour:

  die verschiedenen Rottöne des Gemäldes
  the different reds in the painting

5 Miscellaneous

a) The following words retain the same gender whatever sex of person they refer to:

der Mensch	human being
der Gast	guest
die Geisel	hostage
die Person	person
die Wache	guard
die Waise	orphan
das Genie	genius
das Individuum	individual

das Staatsoberhaupt	head of state
das Opfer	victim
das Mitglied	member

b) Compound nouns have the gender of the final component:

die Urlaubsreise
holiday trip

c) *For adjectival nouns see* **section 4** *above.*

d) Some nouns can have more than one gender:

der Joghurt	**das Joghurt**	**die Joghurt** *(colloquial)*
yoghurt	yoghurt	yoghurt
der Teil	**das Teil**	
part	part, component	

Note that compounds with -teil have only one gender:

der Vorteil	*but*	**das Gegenteil**
advantage		disadvantage

e) The following are the most common nouns which change meaning according to gender:

Note that they usually have different plurals according to the gender.

	MASCULINE (der)	FEMININE (die)	NEUTER (das)
Band	book, volume	band *(music)*	tape, tie
Erbe	heir	–	inheritance
Gehalt	content	–	salary
Golf	bay	–	golf
Heide	heathen	heath	–
Hundert	–	100 *(number)*	100 *(amount)*
Hut	hat	protection	–
Junge	boy	–	young animal
Kiefer	jaw	pine tree	–
Kunde	customer	news	–
Laster	lorry	–	vice

Leiter	leader	ladder	–
Mangel	lack	mangle	–
Maß	–	beer measure	measurement
Mensch	human	–	tart (*insult*)
Moment	moment (*time*)	–	moment (*physics*)
Otter	otter	viper	–
Pack	stack	–	rabble
Schild	shield	–	sign
See	lake	sea	–
Steuer	–	tax	steering wheel
Stift	pin, pencil	–	foundation
Tau	dew	–	rope
Tausend	–	1000 (*number*)	1000 (*amount*)
Tor	fool	–	gate, goal
Verdienst	income	–	merit
Weise	wise man	manner, tune	–

B THE FORMATION OF PLURALS

There are five main plural forms in German; three also sometimes
have an umlaut on the stem vowel. These five forms are set out
below with indications of the main types of nouns to which they
apply. However, plural forms should be learnt together with the
nouns.

1 No plural ending; some add an umlaut

Taken by: Masculine and neuter nouns ending in -chen, -el, -en, -er,
-lein

das Mädchen	die Mädchen	girl
der Hobel	die Hobel	plane (*carpentry*)
das Kabel	die Kabel	cable
der Braten	die Braten	roast
das Kissen	die Kissen	cushion

der Bagger	die Bagger	digger
das Messer	die Messer	knife
das Büchlein	die Büchlein	little book

Some masculine and occasional feminine and neuter nouns take an umlaut:

der Vogel	die Vögel	bird
der Laden	die Läden	shop
der Hammer	die Hämmer	hammer
das Kloster	die Klöster	monastery
die Mutter	die Mütter	mother
die Tochter	die Töchter	daughter

2 Plural ending -e

Taken by: Most masculine nouns, many neuter nouns, a group of common feminine nouns of one syllable and the few feminines ending in -nis; the s is doubled after a -nis ending.

der Tag	die Tage	day
der Freund	die Freunde	friend
der Dom	die Dome	cathedral
der Monat	die Monate	month
der Bericht	die Berichte	report
das Haar	die Haare	hair
das Pfund	die Pfunde	pound
das Gesetz	die Gesetze	law
das Ereignis	die Ereignisse	event
die Kenntnis	die Kenntnisse	knowledge

All feminine monosyllables, many masculine monosyllables and some masculine words formed with prefix + monosyllable take an umlaut:

die Hand	die Hände	hand
die Kunst	die Künste	art
der Traum	die Träume	dream

der Knopf	die Knöpfe	button
der Einwand	die Einwände	objection
der Anfang	die Anfänge	beginning
Note:	das Floß die Flöße	raft

3 Plural ending -(e)n

> ### Note
> The e is included after words ending in -ei, -au, and consonants
> except for -el, -er endings; otherwise the ending is -n; the n is
> doubled after -in endings.

Taken by: A great many feminine nouns, a number of masculine
nouns, and a small number of neuter monosyllables. None take an
umlaut:

die Eitelkeit	die Eitelkeiten	vanity
die Hoffnung	die Hoffnungen	hope
die Ärztin	die Ärztinnen	doctor
die Bäckerei	die Bäckereien	bakery
die Au	die Auen	meadow
die Bahn	die Bahnen	railway
die Straße	die Straßen	street
die Schüssel	die Schüsseln	bowl
die Feder	die Federn	feather
der Mensch	die Menschen	human
der Nerv	die Nerven	nerve
das Bett	die Betten	bed

4 Plural ending -er

Taken by: A good number of neuter nouns, especially
monosyllables, nouns ending in -tum, and a few masculine
monosyllables. All take an umlaut if possible:

das Rad	die Räder	wheel
das Land	die Länder	country
das Lied	die Lieder	song
das Gespenst	die Gespenster	ghost
das Bistum	die Bistümer	bishopric
der Reichtum	die Reichtümer	wealth
der Strauch	die Sträucher	bush
der Geist	die Geister	spirit

5 Plural ending -s

Taken by: Many foreign nouns, especially from English and French,
nouns ending with a single vowel (except -e), abbreviations, proper
names, a few technical terms to do with the weather and the sea.
None take an umlaut:

das Team	die Teams	team
die City	die Citys	city centre
das Brikett	die Briketts	coal briquette
das Sofa	die Sofas	sofa
der Uhu	die Uhus	owl
ein Sozi	die Sozis	socialist
der Pulli	die Pullis	pullover
der Lkw	die Lkws	lorry
Frau/Herr Müller	die Müllers	the Müllers
das Tief	die Tiefs	depression (weather)
das Deck	die Decks	deck

Note that all words deriving from English and ending in -y form
their plural with ys:

das Baby	die Babys

6 Double plurals

Some nouns have two plural forms which are different in meaning; those given below are the commonest:

die Bank	die Bänke	bench
	die Banken	bank
der Bau	die Baue	animal's lair
	die Bauten	building
die Mutter	die Mütter	mother
	die Muttern	nut (*for bolt*)
der Strauß	die Strauße	ostrich
	die Sträuße	bouquet
das Wort	die Wörter	single words
	die Worte	words (*in a sentence*)

Note that the nouns with double gender listed on **p 44-5** above will also have a different plural form for each gender.

7 Singular or plural?

Whilst almost all nouns have both singular and plural forms, some occur only in the singular and a few only in the plural. Usage here is not always the same as in English; consult a dictionary if in doubt.

a) *nouns only occurring in the singular:*

　i) names of substances:

das Fleisch	**das Gummi**	**die Milch**
meat	rubber	milk
die Butter	**das Leder**	**der Schnee**
butter	leather	snow

Note

- These often form plurals by being compounded with either
  -sorten or -arten:

  verschiedene Buttersorten   **zwei Getreidearten**
  different types of butter   two kinds of grain

- Singular is sometimes used for plural:

  zwei Bier, bitte
  two beers, please

ii) many collectives:

das Vieh	**die Bourgeoisie**	**die Polizei**
cattle	the bourgeoisie	the police
das Gepäck	**der Schmuck**	**das Publikum**
luggage	jewellery	the audience

iii) many abstract nouns:

der Fleiß	**die Hitze**	**der Aufbau**
diligence	heat	building up

Note

- Some abstract nouns can also be used in a specific as well as
  a general sense. In these cases they have a plural, eg der Spaß
  (enjoyment) has no plural, but der Spaß (joke) has the plural die
  Späße.

- Abstracts often have parallel forms which can be put into the
  plural, eg der Rat (advice) has no plural, but der Ratschlag (piece
  of advice) has the plural die Ratschläge.

iv) names of colours:

das Schwarz	**das Grün**	**das Blau**
black	green	blue

Note that names for colours formed from the adjective with no ending can be used in the singular with plural meaning, eg die zwei Grün ('the two greens') (*see also* **section A4c**).

v) nouns formed from adjectives (*see* **section A4** *above*) when they do not refer to people and nouns formed from infinitives when they refer to an activity and not to an object:

das Beste ('the best thing') has no plural but die Beste ('the best woman') has the plural die Besten.
das Schreiben ('the act of writing') has no plural but das Schreiben ('the letter') has the plural die Schreiben.

b) *nouns only occurring in the plural:*

i) some geographical names:

die Niederlande
the Netherlands

ii) a few nouns of a collective nature:

die Eltern	**die Leute**	**die Ferien**
parents	people	holidays
die Kosten	**die Antiquitäten**	**die Möbel**
costs	antiques	furniture

Note that modern German sometimes uses the awkward singular

der Elternteil
parent

C CASES

There are four cases in German: nominative, accusative, genitive and dative. They are indicated by systems of endings (called declensions) on any articles or adjectives preceding the noun. There are also a few endings on nouns, as set out below.

The purpose of the cases is to indicate the relationship between nouns and other elements of the sentence or, alternatively, a noun's function in the sentence.

1 The nominative

a) *as the subject of verbs:*

   der Mittelstürmer schießt
   the centre forward shoots

b) *after the verbs* sein, werden, bleiben, heißen, sich betrachten als, sich nennen, *and some other similar verbs where the noun complement to the verb is regarded as being in apposition to the subject:*

   er nennt sich mein Freund
   he calls himself *my friend*

2 The accusative

a) *as the object of verbs:*

   der Schiedsrichter gab einen Elfmeter
   the referee gave *a penalty*

b) *after certain prepositions:* (see pp 201-13)

c) *in certain adverbial phrases, especially of time:*

   er sitzt den ganzen Tag herum
   he just sits around *all day*

d) *the so-called absolute accusative (literary usage):*

   den Mantel um die Schultern, ging er hinaus
   his coat over his shoulders, he went out

3 The genitive

a) *to express possession and similar relationships between two nouns:*

das Büro seines Chefs   **die Reparatur des Wagens**
his boss's office   the repair *of the car*

Note that this is very often used in contexts where the English genitive is also used.

b) *in certain adverbial phrases:*

eines Tages   **meines Erachtens**
one day   in my opinion

c) *after certain prepositions:* (*see* pp 213–16)

d) *when dependent on certain adjectives:*

er ist sich seiner Verantwortung bewusst
he is aware *of his responsibility*

4 The dative

a) *as the indirect object:*

er gab seiner Frau den Brief
he gave the letter *to his wife*

Note that by no means all German verbs that 'take the dative' are obvious from their English equivalents:

er folgte dem Verbrecher
he followed *the criminal*

b) *after certain prepositions:* (*see* pp 196–200, 203–13, 215–6)

c) *when dependent on certain adjectives:*

sie ist ihrer Mutter sehr ähnlich
she is very like *her mother*

D THE DECLENSION OF NOUNS

All masculine and neuter nouns end in -(e)s in the genitive singular.

Some masculine and neuter nouns, mostly monosyllables, can take an -e ending in the dative singular. This is optional and is normally used for reasons of rhythm. There are a few idiomatic expressions where it is required, eg im Grunde ('basically').

All nouns end in -n in the dative plural, except those forming the plural with -s.

1 Masculine

	SINGULAR	PLURAL	
nom	der Vater	die Väter	father
acc	den Vater	die Väter	
gen	des Vaters	der Väter	
dat	dem Vater	den Vätern	
nom	der Tag	die Tage	day
acc	den Tag	die Tage	
gen	des Tag(e)s	der Tage	
dat	dem Tag(e)	den Tagen	

a) A group of masculine nouns, often called weak nouns, takes the ending -(e)n in all cases apart from the nominative singular:

	SINGULAR	PLURAL	
nom	der Löwe	die Löwen	lion
acc	den Löwen	die Löwen	
gen	des Löwen	der Löwen	
dat	dem Löwen	den Löwen	
nom	der Christ	die Christen	Christian
acc	den Christen	die Christen	
gen	des Christen	der Christen	
dat	dem Christen	den Christen	

nom	der Student	die Studenten	student
acc	den Studenten	die Studenten	
gen	des Studenten	der Studenten	
dat	dem Studenten	den Studenten	
nom	der Herr	die Herren	gentleman
acc	den Herrn	die Herren	
gen	des Herr(e)n	der Herren	
dat	dem Herrn	den Herren	

Masculine nouns which have -(e)n endings in the singular consist of:

i) nouns ending in -e denoting humans or animals:

der Erbe	**der Zeuge**
heir	witness
der Bulgare	**der Biologe**
Bulgarian	biologist

ii) a number of monosyllables ending with a consonant and denoting humans or animals:

der Bär	**der Fürst**	**der Held**
bear	prince	hero
der Mensch	**der Narr**	**der Prinz**
human	fool	prince
der Zar		
Tsar		
plus	**der Bauer**	**der Nachbar**
	farmer	neighbour

iii) words derived from foreign words with endings such as -ant, -ent, -graph, -ist and others; most, but not all, are names for human occupations:

der Emigrant	**der Polizist**	**der Bürokrat**
emigré	policeman	bureaucrat
der Astronom	**der Automat**	**der Athlet**
astronomer	vending machine	athlete

der Doktorand	**der Fotograf**	**der Pilot**
PhD candidate	photographer	pilot
der Bandit		
bandit		

b) A small number of masculine nouns end in -(e)n in the plural and in the accusative and dative singular but form the genitive singular by adding -(e)ns; das Herz is similar except for the accusative singular:

	SINGULAR	**PLURAL**	
nom	**der Name**	**die Namen**	name
acc	**den Namen**	**die Namen**	
gen	**des Namens**	**der Namen**	
dat	**dem Namen**	**den Namen**	
nom	**das Herz**	**die Herzen**	heart
acc	**das Herz**	**die Herzen**	
gen	**des Herzens**	**der Herzen**	
dat	**dem Herzen**	**den Herzen**	

Similar to this is: **der Buchstabe** letter *(of alphabet)*

c) There is a small group of words with a double form in the nominative which take -ns in the genitive singular whichever nominative form is used:

der Friede/Frieden	**der Funke/Funken**
peace	spark
der Gedanke/Gedanken	**der Glaube/Glauben**
thought	belief
der Same/Samen	**der Wille/Willen**
seed	will *(determination)*

	SINGULAR	**PLURAL**	
nom	**der Funke(n)**	**die Funken**	spark
acc	**den Funken**	**die Funken**	
gen	**des Funkens**	**der Funken**	
dat	**dem Funken**	**den Funken**	

2 Feminine

	SINGULAR	PLURAL	
nom	die Frau	die Frauen	woman
acc	die Frau	die Frauen	
gen	der Frau	der Frauen	
dat	der Frau	den Frauen	

nom	die Nacht	die Nächte	night
acc	die Nacht	die Nächte	
gen	der Nacht	der Nächte	
dat	der Nacht	den Nächten	

3 Neuter

	SINGULAR	PLURAL	
nom	das Gebäude	die Gebäude	building
acc	das Gebäude	die Gebäude	
gen	des Gebäudes	der Gebäude	
dat	dem Gebäude	den Gebäuden	

nom	das Gras	die Gräser	grass
acc	das Gras	die Gräser	
gen	des Grases	der Gräser	
dat	dem Gras(e)	den Gräsern	

4 Miscellaneous notes on forms

a) *-s or -es in genitive?*

i) **-es** is always added after words ending in -s, -ß, -x, -z, -sch:

der Krebs	**des Krebses**	**der Sitz**	**des Sitzes**
crab		seat	
der Kitsch	**des Kitsches**		
kitsch			

ii) **-es** is often added after a word which ends with a double consonant:

der Kopf	**des Kopfes**	**das Hemd**	**des Hemdes**
head		shirt	

iii) -es is always added to

Gott	**Gottes**
God	

iv) -s is normally added to words ending with an unstressed syllable:

der Anfang	**des Anfangs**
beginning	

v) -s is normally added to words ending with a vowel or vowel + h:

das Kino	**des Kinos**	**der Schuh**	**des Schuhs**
cinema		shoe	

vi) -s is added to most foreign nouns and to nouns of colour:

das Restaurant	**des Restaurants**	**das Rot**	**des Rots**
restaurant		red	

vii) foreign words ending in -as, -os, -us have no extra ending in the genitive singular:

der Mythos	**des Mythos**	**der**	**des**
myth		**Kommunismus**	**Kommunismus**
		communism	

b) Neuter nouns ending in -nis double the -s before the genitive ending:

das Bildnis	**des Bildnisses**
portrait	

5 The Saxon Genitive

The so-called Saxon genitive in which the genitive word comes first is used for proper names (*see* section 6 *below*), eg Bachs Kantaten. Otherwise it is uncommon but is sometimes used in literary style:

des Tages Hitze
the heat of the day

6 The genitive of proper names and titles

a) All names take an -s ending in the genitive, whether masculine or feminine:

Pauls Vater	**Monikas Freund**
Paul's father	Monika's friend

i) Names consisting of more than one element take the -s on the last part:

die Stücke Friedrich Dürrenmatts
Friedrich Dürrenmatt's plays

Exceptions are some medieval names:

die Werke Walthers von der Vogelweide
Walther von der Vogelweide's works

ii) Names ending in -s, -ß, -x, -z cannot be dealt with in this way. The addition of -ens (eg Fritzens) was common but is now felt to be old-fashioned. The addition of an apostrophe after the -s is still sometimes used in written German (eg Grass' Stücke – 'Grass's plays'), but in general the problem is avoided by using von or des/der:

der Einfluss von Marx   **die Reise des Kolumbus**
Marx's influence   Columbus's voyage

iii) The genitive -s is omitted when the proper name is preceded by an article in the genitive:

die Zeugnisse der Luise
Luise's school reports

b) When a name is preceded by a title, only the name takes the -s:

die Politik Präsident Bushs   **Tante Friedas Schmuck**
President Bush's policies   Aunt Frieda's jewellery
but: Herr is always declined (in the accusative and dative as well):
Herrn Köpkes Angebot   **Herrn Professor Winters Aufsatz**
Mr Köpke's offer   Professor Winter's essay
ein Brief an Herrn Doktor Schmidt
a letter to Doctor Schmidt

Note that letters should be addressed to Herrn X; the word an is often put before, but is always understood anyway.

c) After statt, trotz, wegen neither title nor name is declined:

trotz Peter **wegen Direktor Braun**
in spite of Peter because of the director, Mr Braun

d) When preceded by an article, a demonstrative or possessive neither title nor name is now generally declined:

das Schwert des General Herder
General Herder's sword

e) Additional titles coming after the name are always declined:

die Abdankung Eduards des Achten
the abdication of Edward VIII

das Leben Peters des Großen
the life of Peter the Great

4 ADJECTIVES

Adjectives are describing words which usually accompany a noun (or a pronoun) and tell us what someone or something is like:

ein kleines Dorf
a little village

meine Jacke ist blau
my jacket is blue

der neue Film
the new film

es war fantastisch
it was fantastic

 A AGREEMENT

1 Use

There is a major difference between English and German in the predicative use of adjectives (eg after 'is', 'are', 'were') and their attributive use (before nouns and pronouns). In the sentences

PREDICATIVE		ATTRIBUTIVE
my car is old	*and*	I drive an old car

the word 'old' appears twice, in identical form. But in the German sentences

mein Wagen ist alt	*and*	**ich fahre einen alten Wagen**
my car is old		I drive an old car

the word **alt** appears once with and once without an ending.

The predicative use is so similar to English that it should not be a problem. However, German adjectives used attributively can prove troublesome, since only one of a number of endings is ever correct in a given context. The rules governing these endings are set out below, but first here are some more examples to illustrate this important difference:

PREDICATIVE	**ATTRIBUTIVE**
das Boot ist neu	**ich brauche ein neues Boot**
the boat is new	I need a new boat
seine Eltern waren reich	**er kam mit seinen reichen Eltern nicht aus**
his parents were rich	he couldn't get on with his rich parents

2 Endings

The endings of an attributive adjective in German are determined by the noun which follows it, according to three factors:

a) its gender (whether masculine, feminine or neuter)

b) its number (is it singular or plural?)

c) its case (nominative, accusative *etc*)

In addition, there are variations, depending on whether the adjectives comes after

a) a definite article (der, die, das *etc*)

b) an indefinite article (ein, eine *etc*)

or

c) is not preceded by any article, pronoun or possessive adjective.

3 Participles as adjectives

a) Present participles may be used as attributive adjectives:

ein weinendes Baby	**bellende Hunde**
a crying baby	barking dogs

They can also be used in adjectival phrases:

das gerade vorbeifahrende Auto
the car that's just driving past

b) Past participles may be used both attributively (as an adjective and in a phrase) and predicatively:

die verlorene Stadt
the lost city

das Geschirr ist abgewaschen
the dishes are washed

die Reparatur der beschädigten Teile
the repair of the damaged parts

4 Exceptions

In some cases, the form of certain adjectives does not change, no matter what precedes them or what the gender, number or case of the following noun may be. These exceptions are:

a) *the adjective form of town names:*

wer liest die Londoner Times?
who reads the London Times?

wir treffen uns in einem Glasgower Lokal
we're meeting in a Glasgow pub

b) halb *and* ganz *with towns, countries and continents:*

in ganz Hamburg
throughout Hamburg

ganz Schottland
the whole of Scotland

but

die ganze Schweiz
the whole of Switzerland

(*For the use of the article, see* **Articles A2**)

c) rosa, lila *and* prima:

ein rosa/lila Kleid
a pink/lilac dress

eine prima Idee
a great idea

Note that adjectives ending in -el and -er drop the e before the l or r when they are used attributively:

dunkel
dark

ein dunkler Anzug
a dark suit

teuer
expensive

eine teure Kamera
an expensive camera

5 Adjectives relating to countries

Adjectives formed from the names of countries or continents are written with an initial lower case letter, not a capital:

italienisches Eis
Italian ice-cream

die französische Hauptstadt
the French capital

6 Adjectives deriving from proper names

Adjectives formed from proper names ending in -(i)sch are now written with an initial lower case letter:

das brechtsche Theater
the Brechtian theatre

 B ADJECTIVE ENDINGS

1 After the definite article (der, die, das)

	MASCULINE	FEMININE	NEUTER	PLURAL ALL GENDERS
nom	-e	-e	-e	-en
acc	-en	-e	-e	-en
gen	-en	-en	-en	-en
dat	-en	-en	-en	-en

Examples:

a) *nominative*

   Masc Sing

der alte Mann wohnt hier
the old man lives here

   Fem Sing

die neue Rektorin heißt Ulrike
the new headmistress is called Ulrike

Neut Sing

das grüne Kleid ist besonders schick
the green dress is extremely chic

Plural

die blauen Fahrräder kosten mehr
the blue bicycles cost more

b) *accusative*

Masc Sing

haben Sie den alten Mann gesehen?
have you seen the old man?

Fem Sing

ich kenne die neue Rektorin schon
I already know the new headmistress

Neut Sing

niemand hat das grüne Kleid gekauft
no-one has bought the green dress

Plural

wo kann man die blauen Fahrräder bekommen?
where can one get the blue bicycles?

c) *genitive*

Masc Sing

das sind die Kinder des alten Mannes
those are the old man's children

Fem Sing

das Büro der neuen Rektorin ist rechts
the new headmistress's office is on the right

Neut Sing

der Preis des grünen Kleid(e)s ist zu hoch
the price of the green dress is too high

> *Plural*
>
> **kennen Sie den Hersteller der blauen Fahrräder?**
> do you know who manufactures the blue bicycles?

d) *dative*

> *Masc Sing*
>
> **die Nachbarn helfen dem alten Mann**
> the neighbours help the old man

> *Fem Sing*
>
> **wir verstehen uns gut mit der neuen Rektorin**
> we get on well with the new headmistress

> *Neut Sing*
>
> **im grünen Kleid sehen Sie gut aus**
> you look good in the green dress

> *Plural*
>
> **mit den blauen Fahrrädern habe ich viel Erfolg**
> I'm having a lot of success with the blue bicycles

Note that adjectives used after the following words take the same endings as for the definite article:

der/die/dasjenige	the
der/die/dasselbe	the same
dieser, diese, dieses	this
irgendwelcher	some (or other)
jeder, jede, jedes	each
jener, jene, jenes	that
mancher, manche, manches	many a
solcher, solche, solches	such
welcher?, welche?, welches?	which?
alle *(pl)*	all
beide *(pl)*	both

2 After the indefinite article

	MASCULINE	FEMININE	NEUTER
nom	-er	-e	-es
acc	-en	-e	-es
gen	-en	-en	-en
dat	-en	-en	-en

Examples:

a) *nominative:*

> *Masc Sing*

> **ein deutscher Film läuft heute im Kino**
> there's a German film on today at the cinema

> *Fem Sing*

> **eine kleine Stadt liegt nicht weit von hier**
> there's a little town not far from here

> *Neut Sing*

> **ein weißes Kaninchen wäre ein schönes Geschenk!**
> a white rabbit would be a lovely present!

b) *accusative*

> *Masc Sing*

> **einen deutschen Film sieht man nicht oft**
> you don't often get the chance to see a German film

> *Fem Sing*

> **das braucht eine halbe Stunde**
> that will take half an hour

> *Neut Sing*

> **hast du ein neues Radio?**
> have you got a new radio?

ADJECTIVES —————————————————————————————————

c) *genitive*

> *Masc Sing*

der Titel eines deutschen Film(e)s
the title of a German film

> *Fem Sing*

im Laufe einer schlaflosen Nacht
in the course of a sleepless night

> *Neut Sing*

das Foto eines alten Schlosses
the photo of an old castle

d) *dative*

> *Masc Sing*

man unterhielt die Besucher mit einem deutschen Film
the visitors were entertained with a German film

> *Fem Sing*

nach einer langen Pause
after a long pause

> *Neut Sing*

außer einem langweiligen Fußballspiel war nichts los
apart from a boring game of football there was nothing happening

---

Note

- In addition, adjectives used after the following words take the same endings as above, when used in the singular:

irgendein/eine/ein	**kein, keine, kein**
some (or other)	no

  also all possessive adjectives, eg **mein** (my), **Ihr** (your).

- After **keine** and possessive adjectives in the plural, all adjectives end in -en, whatever case they are used in (*see* **section B1**).

3 Without any preceding article

	MASCULINE	FEMININE	NEUTER	PLURAL ALL GENDERS
nom	-er	-e	-es	-e
acc	-en	-e	-es	-e
gen	-en	-er	-en	-er
dat	-em	-er	-em	-en

Examples:

a) *nominative*

> *Masc Sing*

feiner Wein kostet viel
good wine costs a lot

> *Fem Sing*

englische Studentin sucht Arbeit
female English student seeks work

> *Neut Sing*

eiskaltes Wasser schmeckt gut
ice-cold water tastes good

> *Plural*

junge Leute sind besonders willkommen
young people are especially welcome

b) *accusative*

> *Masc Sing*

er hat furchtbaren Hunger
he is incredibly hungry

> *Fem Sing*

Polizei fängt wilde Katze
Police catch wild cat

Neut Sing

ich trinke gern eiskaltes Wasser
I like drinking ice-cold water

Plural

sie hat wunderbare Augen
she's got wonderful eyes

c) *genitive*

Masc Sing

ein Glas guten Wein(e)s genügt (more usual: guter Wein)
one glass of good wine is sufficient

Fem Sing

französischer Herkunft
of French extraction

Neut Sing

der Geschmack selbst gebackenen Brot(e)s
the taste of home-made bread

Plural

der Genuss alkoholischer Getränke
the consumption of alcoholic drinks

d) *dative*

Masc Sing

mit großem Erfolg
with great success

Fem Sing

aus guter Familie
from a good home

Neut Sing

unter lautem Stöhnen
amid loud groans

Plural

im Vergleich zu japanischen Managern
in comparison with Japanese managers

Note the following points:

i) In addition, adjectives used after the following words take the same endings as above:

singular only

ein bisschen	**ein wenig**	**solch**
a little	a little	such
viel	**wenig**	**welch**
much	little	what!

solch würzigen Käse habe ich noch nie gegessen!
I've never eaten such strong cheese!

unter viel verdientem Beifall verließ sie die Bühne
she left the stage to much deserved applause

singular and plural

mehr	**weniger**	**was für**
more	less, fewer	what (kind of)

mit mehr finanzieller Unterstützung
with more financial support

mit weniger regionalen Zeitungen
with fewer regional newspapers

plural only

einige	**ein paar**	**einzelne**
some	some, a few	individual
mehrere	**viele**	**wenige**
several	many	few

es gibt nur noch ein paar schwierige Fälle
there are just a few difficult cases left

trotz mehrerer strenger Warnungen
despite several stern warnings

numbers
zwei drei vier *etc*

gegen den Rat zweier meiner Freunde
against the advice of two of my friends

ii) After **etwas, mehr, nichts, viel** and **wenig**, but when used without
a following noun, adjectives are written with an initial capital
letter and take the same endings as a neuter noun (*see* **p** 42):

nichts Besonderes ist heute passiert
nothing in particular happened today

wer hat (et)was Interessantes zu berichten?
who has something interesting to report?

er hat in seinem Leben nur wenig Gutes getan
he hasn't done much good in his life

iii) If two adjectives come together before a noun, both take the
same endings:

die Blätter des großen alten Baumes
the leaves of the big old tree

ein Kind mit gutem artigem Benehmen
a well-behaved child

 ## C COMPARATIVES AND SUPERLATIVES

People or things can be compared to others by using:

> **so + adjective + wie**
> as + adjective + as

or

> **ebenso/genauso/geradeso + adjective + wie**
> just as + adjective + as

er ist (eben)so groß wie ich
he is (just) as tall as me/I am

However, when the comparison involves superiority the comparative
and superlative forms of the adjective are used.

Like in English, German adjectives form the comparative by adding
-er and the superlative by adding -st or -est:

klein	**kleiner**	**(der) kleinst(e)**
small	smaller	smallest

This scheme is applied more consistently in German than in
English:

intelligent	**intelligenter**	**(der) intelligentest(e)**
intelligent	more intelligent	most intelligent

1 Comparative adjectives

a) *formation*

i) As with adjectives in their basic form, comparative adjectives
   only take an ending (to indicate gender, number and case)
   when used attributively. These endings (*see* **section B**) are
   added to the standard -er of the comparative:

   die Farbe muss heller sein
   the colour must be lighter

   but:

   wir möchten eine hellere Farbe
   we'd like a lighter colour

   dieses Nilpferd ist so dick!
   this hippo is so fat!

   but:

   ein noch dickeres Nilpferd
   an even fatter hippo

   Note that adjectives ending in -el and -er normally drop the
   e before the l or r when they are used in the comparative:

dieses Zimmer da ist dunkel	**aber dieses hier ist dunkler**
that room is dark	but this one is darker

ii) Some common one-syllable adjectives add an umlaut (and -er) in the comparative. The most common are:

alt	(old)	älter	(older, elder)
arm	(poor)	ärmer	(poorer)
dumm	(stupid)	dümmer	(more stupid)
groß	(big, great)	größer	(bigger, greater)
hart	(hard)	härter	(harder)
jung	(young)	jünger	(younger)
kalt	(cold)	kälter	(colder)
klug	(clever)	klüger	(cleverer)
kurz	(short)	kürzer	(shorter)
lang	(long)	länger	(longer)
schwach	(weak)	schwächer	(weaker)
stark	(strong)	stärker	(stronger)
warm	(warm)	wärmer	(warmer)

ich brauche einen jüngeren Mann!
I need a younger man/husband!

mein Bericht war lang, aber deiner war bestimmt länger
my report was long, but yours was definitely longer

iii) Note the comparative forms of the following:

gut	(good)	besser	(better)
hoch	(high, tall)	höher	(higher, taller)
viel	(much, a lot of)	mehr	(more)

b) *usage*

i) In addition to the attributive use of comparatives:
ich kenne einen kürzeren Weg
I know a shorter way

and the simple predicative use:

Big Ben ist höher
Big Ben is taller

an explicit comparison between two people or things can be made by adding als:

sie bekommt ein höheres Stipendium als ich
she gets a bigger grant than me/than I do

ihre Bibliothek ist älter als unsere
their library is older than ours

ii) Note, however, the set expression denn je:

besser denn je   **weißer denn je**
better than ever   whiter than ever

iii) Note, also, the construction je + comparative, desto/umso + comparative:

je eher, desto besser
the sooner, the better

je heller die Farbe (ist), umso größer (ist) die Wirkung
the lighter the colour (is), the greater the effect

iv) A small number of adjectives can be used in the comparative form without any obvious sense of comparison:

eine ältere Dame   **auf längere Zeit**
an elderly lady   for a while

2 Superlative adjectives

a) *formation*

i) The German superlative adjective is formed by combining the definite article (der/die/das) with an adjective plus suffix -(e)st and an ending.

ii) Superlatives take endings when used both attributively and predicatively. (Compare the basic form of adjectives and comparatives, which only take an ending when used attributively.)

iii) When used attributively, these endings, which are added to the -(e)st suffix, are the same as those in section B1:

die berühmteste Philosophin ihrer Generation
the most famous woman philosopher of her generation

mit dem kostbarsten Ring der Welt
with the most expensive ring in the world

Note that the **e** in adjectives ending in -el and -er is retained in the superlative:

das dunkelste Zimmer von allen
the darkest room of all

iv) The common one-syllable adjectives that add an umlaut in the comparative (*see* section C1) do the same in the superlative.

der älteste Präsident der USA
the oldest President of the USA

v) Note the following irregular forms of the superlative:

gut	(good)	**(der/die/das)** best- *etc*	(best)
hoch	(high, tall)	**(der/die/das)** höchst- *etc*	(highest, tallest)
nah	(near)	**(der/die/das)** nächst- *etc*	(nearest, next)
viel	(much, a lot of)	**(der/die/das)** meist- *etc*	(most)

vi) Another form of the superlative adjective comes from combining **am** and an adjective plus **-(e)sten**:
billig (cheap) **am billigsten** ([the] cheapest)
This construction can only be used predicatively or after the verb:

dieser hier ist am billigsten
this one here is the cheapest

Note that it does not have any endings.

b) *usage*

i) Superlative expressions are often not complete without mention of the people or things which act as a reference group:

das schlechteste Wetter des Sommers
the worst weather of the summer

wer ist die mutigste von euch?
who's the bravest of you (girls/women)?

The words 'des Sommers' or 'von euch' are the reference groups.

If a reference group is mentioned, the form of the superlative adjective with the definite article is the one most commonly used.

ii) If no reference group is mentioned, both the form with the definite article and that with am can be used:

diese Eier sind die billigsten/am billigsten
these eggs are (the) cheapest

er ist einfach der Beste
he's simply the best

iii) A small number of adjectives can be used in the superlative form without any obvious sense of comparison:

es ist höchste Zeit   **im äußersten Fall kostet es 2 Euro**
it's high time   it'll cost 2 euros at the outside

iv) To express 'in' as in phrases like 'the biggest in the world' *etc*, German uses either in or the genitive case:

die größte Stadt Deutschlands/in Deutschland
the biggest town in Germany

v) Note also the following constructions with superlatives:

der meistgesungene Schlager
the most (frequently) sung hit

der meistgenannte Autor
the author mentioned most often

as well as the set expression **bestgehasst** as in:

der bestgehasste Politiker
the most hated politician

5 ADVERBS

There are two main differences between German and English adverbs:

(a) many German adverbs have the same form as the corresponding adjective:

die Wohnung ist billig *(adj)*
the flat is cheap

er lebt billig *(adv)*
he lives cheaply

(b) the word order with adverbs often differs from English:

sie übt oft Klavier
she often practises the piano

er fährt morgen nach Hause
he's going home tomorrow

 A FORMATION

1 Words which are exclusively adverbs

da (there)
da sind sie!
there they are!

sehr (very)
sehr nett
very nice

geradeaus (straight on)
nur geradeaus!
keep straight on!

2 Adverbs identical in form with adjectives

ADJECTIVE
schön (beautiful)
furchtbar (terrible)

ADVERB
schön (beautifully)
furchtbar (terribly)

sie ist schön, und sie singt auch schön
she's beautiful, and she sings beautifully too

er hat furchtbar gespielt – es war wirklich furchtbar, nicht?
he played terribly – it was really terrible, wasn't it?

3 Adverbs formed from participles

sie spricht zögernd
she speaks hesitantly

übertrieben groß
exaggeratedly large

4 Adverbs formed from other parts of speech plus suffix

a) -lich

ADJECTIVE
neu (new, recent)
kurz (short)

ADVERB
neulich (recently)
kürzlich (recently)

kürzlich bekamen sie einen Computer
they recently got a computer

b) -mal(s)

ADJECTIVE *or* **NUMERAL**
jed- (every)
manch- (many a)
ein- (one)
mehr- (several)

ADVERB
jedes Mal (every time)
manchmal (sometimes)
einmal (once)
mehrmals (several times)

er hat nur einmal geklopft
he only knocked once

c) -ermaßen

ADJECTIVE
einig- (some)
folgend- (following)

ADVERB
einigermaßen (somewhat)
folgendermaßen (as follows)

ich war einigermaßen überrascht
I was somewhat surprised

d) -s

NOUN
(der) Mittag (midday)
(der) Freitag (Friday)

ADVERB
mittags (at midday)
freitags (on Fridays)

mittags isst er in der Kantine
at midday he eats in the canteen

e) **-(er)weise**

-weise can be added to the end of some nouns, -erweise to the
end of some adjectives:

NOUN or **ADJECTIVE**	**ADVERB**
(der) Teil (part)	**teilweise** (partly, in parts)
begreiflich (understandable)	**begreiflicherweise** (understandably)

Ihr Aufsatz ist nur teilweise gut
your essay is only good in parts

das ist normalerweise nicht der Fall
that's not normally the case

B USAGE

Adverbs are often used to qualify a verb, but as adverbial
intensifiers they can also qualify adjectives and other adverbs.

1 With a verb

morgen schreibt er   **verlassen Sie uns hier?**
he'll write tomorrow   are you leaving us here?

German usage makes a consistent distinction between position and
movement in relation to adverbs. For native speakers of English the
greatest difficulty is in translating 'here', 'there' and 'where?'.

wir wohnen hier we live here	*but:*	**sie fährt hierher** she's driving here (= to here)
sie saß da/dort she was sitting there	*but:*	**er lief dahin/dorthin** he ran there (= to there)
wo arbeiten Sie? where do you work?	*but:*	**wohin fliegen Sie?** where are you flying (to)?
wo wartet er? where is he waiting?	*but:*	**woher kommt er?** where does he come from?

Note that in conversation the suffixes -hin and -her often go to the end of the clause:

da gehen wir nie hin!
we never go there!

wo kommen Sie her?
where do you come from?

2 With an adjective

das ist fast einmalig
that's almost unique

es war unglaublich kalt
it was unbelievably cold

ein sehr langweiliges Buch
a very boring book

3 With another adverb

ich koche ebenso gut
I cook just as well

er schreibt erstaunlich schnell
he writes amazingly quickly

atme schön tief!
breathe nice and deeply!

C WORD ORDER

1 Qualifying an adjective or another adverb

Adverbs come immediately before the adjective or adverb they qualify:

sehr gut
very good/well

immer länger
longer and longer

viel lieber
much rather

but: **gut genug**
good enough

ganz hoch
quite tall/high

äußerst dünn
extremely thin(ly)

weiter rechts
further (along) on the right

2 Qualifying a verb

a) In statements the normal position of the adverb is at the end of the clause, but before a past participle, infinitive, separable prefix and, in a subordinate clause, before the finite verb:

Herr Braun liest nicht oft   **sie hat neulich geschrieben**
Mr Braun doesn't read much   she wrote recently
ich weiß, dass er das Geschenk morgen bringt
I know he'll bring the present tomorrow

Note that adverbs of time often occur before a noun in the accusative case:

wir haben heute unsere Weihnachtskarten geschrieben
we've written our Christmas cards today

b) In direct questions the order of the subject and finite verb is reversed, but the normal position of the adverb otherwise remains as in a):

liest Herr Braun nicht oft?   **hat sie neulich geschrieben?**
doesn't Mr Braun often read?   has she written recently?

In indirect questions the position of an adverb in the subordinate clause is as in a):

er hat gefragt, ob sie neulich geschrieben hat
he asked if she had written recently

c) In a simple command the normal position of the adverb is after Sie and wir, or after the finite verb (in the case of the du and ihr forms of the imperative):

bleiben Sie da!   **gehen wir morgen baden!**
stay there!   let's go swimming tomorrow!
fahr langsamer!   **esst schnell euer Frühstück!**
drive more slowly!   eat your breakfast quickly!

3 Sequence of Adverbs

a) When two or more adverbs (or adverbial phrases) appear in the
same sentence, they usually do so in the following sequence:

1) TIME
2) MANNER
3) PLACE

ich bleibe oft alleine zu Hause
I often stay at home by myself

wer fährt diesen Sommer per Anhalter ins Ausland?
who's going hitching abroad this summer?

joggen wir jetzt schnell durch den Park
let's jog quickly through the park now

If a cause or reason is included it usually occurs after an
expression of time:

er ist gestern Abend wegen der Kälte früh ins Bett gegangen
he went to bed early last night because of the cold

Note that with two expressions of time, the more general one
comes first:

sie kommen morgen um 5 Uhr an
they're arriving at 5 o'clock tomorrow

b) If several adverbial items are used, it is common for one to be
placed at the beginning of the sentence. This may be for special
emphasis or for stylistic reasons, since a long string of items can
be cumbersome.

Compare:

**letzten Montag hat sie ihn aus Eifersucht mit einem Hammer in ihrem
Schlafzimmer getötet**
last Monday she killed him out of jealousy with a hammer in her
bedroom

with

aus Eifersucht hat sie ihn letzten Montag mit einem Hammer in ihrem Schlafzimmer getötet
it was out of jealousy that she killed him last Monday with a hammer in her bedroom

and

mit einem Hammer hat sie ihn letzten Montag aus Eifersucht in ihrem Schlafzimmer getötet

and

in ihrem Schlafzimmer hat sie ihn letzten Montag aus Eifersucht mit einem Hammer getötet

D COMPARATIVES AND SUPERLATIVES

1 Comparative adverbs

a) Comparative adverbs, like comparative adjectives, are formed by adding -er to the standard form. This only applies to adverbs with the same standard form as adjectives:

ADVERB	COMPARATIVE ADVERB
einfach (simply)	**einfacher** (more simply)
selten (rarely)	**seltener** (more rarely)
umstritten (controversially)	**umstrittener** (more controversially)

könnten Sie das bitte etwas einfacher ausdrücken?
could you put that a bit more simply, please?

heutzutage kommt das seltener vor
nowadays that happens more rarely

Note that the comparative form of gern is lieber:

ich trinke gern Cola, aber ich trinke lieber Tee
I like drinking coke, but I prefer to drink tea

For other irregular forms see Adjectives section C1.

b) 'than' is translated by als:

er läuft schneller als sein Bruder
he runs faster than his brother

c) immer + comparative renders the English double comparative:

seine Stimme klingt immer unangenehmer
his voice sounds more and more unpleasant

sie bleibt immer länger von zu Hause weg
she stays for longer and longer periods away from home

d) 'even' and 'all the' are translated by noch and umso:

jetzt besuchen sie uns noch häufiger als im Vorjahr
they now visit us even more frequently than last year

nach einer Pause werden wir umso besser arbeiten können
we'll be able to work all the better if we take a rest

2 Superlative adverbs

a) Superlative adverbs are formed by combining am with an adverb plus the ending -(e)sten. This only applies in the case of adverbs with the same standard form as adjectives:

ADVERB	SUPERLATIVE ADVERB
blöd (stupidly)	**am blödsten** (most stupidly)
selten (rarely)	**am seltensten** (most rarely)
elegant (elegantly)	**am elegantesten** (most elegantly)

von allen hat sie sich am blödsten benommen
she behaved most stupidly of all

die Drossel kommt am seltensten
the thrush comes the most rarely

Note that the superlative form of gern is am liebsten:

ich reite gern, fahre aber am liebsten Rad
I like riding, but like cycling best

b) When 'most' in English means 'very', rather than implying a
comparison, it is usually translated by höchst, äußerst or sehr:

höchst unwahrscheinlich   **äußerst dankbar**
most unlikely   most grateful

das war sehr nett von Ihnen!
that was most kind of you!

6 PRONOUNS

Pronouns are words which can substitute for nouns. They are divided into personal, reflexive, indefinite, relative and interrogative pronouns.

A PERSONAL PRONOUNS

1 Forms

	NOMINATIVE	ACCUSATIVE	GENITIVE	DATIVE
I	ich	mich	meiner	mir
you	du	dich	deiner	dir
he	er	ihn	seiner	ihm
she	sie	sie	ihrer	ihr
it	es	es	seiner	ihm
we	wir	uns	unser	uns
you	ihr	euch	euer	euch
you	Sie	Sie	Ihrer	Ihnen
they	sie	sie	ihrer	ihnen

2 The translation of 'you'

du is used for the singular when talking to family, friends, children and animals; ihr is used for the plural. Sie is used when talking to people with whom you are not on 'du' terms. Nowadays young people often address each other by 'du' or 'ihr' even when they are not acquainted. A group containing a mixture of people you would call du and those you would call Sie can quite properly be addressed by ihr even though you would revert to Sie when talking to one individual. God and saints are addressed by du.

hast du die Hausaufgaben?	**seid ihr schon zu Hause?**
have you got your homework?	are you home already?
wie heißen Sie, bitte?	**rechts sehen Sie das Schloss**
what is your name, please?	on the right you can see the castle

3 The use of cases

a) *the nominative*

The nominative is used for the subjects of verbs and following the verb sein:

ich sehe	**kannst du kommen?**
I see	can you come?

ich bin es	**das sind wir**	**morgen gehen wir**
it's me	that's us	we're going tomorrow

b) *the accusative*

The accusative is used for the direct object of verbs and after certain prepositions (*see also* pp 201-13)

ich mag ihn	**nimm uns mit!**	**ein Brief an dich**
I like him	take us too	a letter to you

Note the use of an accusative object in wie ('such as') clauses where it is not used in English:

das sind Berge, wie es sie in meiner Heimat gibt
they are mountains such as we have at home

c) *the genitive*

The genitive form of pronouns is rare and is only used with a small number of verbs, prepositions (*see also* pp 213-16) and adjectives which are followed by the genitive:

er war ihrer satt	**trotz seiner**
he was tired of her	in spite of him
erinnerst du dich meiner?	
do you remember me?	

d) *the dative*

The dative is used for the indirect object of verbs and after certain prepositions (*see pp 196-200, 203-13 and 215-6*):

ich gebe es dir
I'm giving it to you

nach Ihnen
after you

folgen Sie ihr!
follow her

bei uns
at our house

4 Gender

Pronouns take the gender of the noun they replace. This means that English 'it' will often be translated by er or sie:

wirf den Stuhl weg, er ist alt
throw the chair away, it's old

diese Tasche ist billig, kauf sie doch!
that bag is cheap, go on, buy it

When a noun that refers to people does not have natural gender, there is no change in gender with the pronoun:

und das Kind? – es kommt mit
and the child? – he's/she's coming too

er sah das Opfer, wie es weggetragen wurde
he saw the victim being carried away

but:

das Mädchen may be referred to as either es or sie, the latter especially if grown up:

das Mädchen, das dort tanzt, kennst du sie?
do you know the girl who's dancing there?

Note the corresponding use of the possessive adjective sein:

das Mädchen spielte mit seiner Puppe
the girl was playing with her doll

5 Special uses of es

a) es can be used as an introductory subject when the noun which is the real subject comes after the verb. Whether the verb is singular or plural depends on the noun. This use sometimes corresponds to the English 'there was ...':

es stand ein Mann vor dem Haus
there was a man standing outside the house

es tanzten viele Kinder
a lot of children were dancing

When es is used in this way with sein it must be remembered that, unlike in English, the verb will be singular or plural depending on the noun following:

es ist deine Freundin   **es sind meine Eltern**
it's your girlfriend   it's my parents

Note that with a noun es comes before the verb, but with a pronoun the order must be pronoun + verb + es:

ach, ihr seid's   **ich bin es**
oh, it's you   it's me

b) es is used as the object of sagen and tun where the English equivalent is 'so':

du hast es gesagt   **ich hoffe, es zu tun**
you said so   I hope to do so

c) es is used after the verb sein to refer back to a noun or adjective in a preceding clause where in English the verb 'to be' stands alone:

dieser soll besser sein; meinst du, dass er es ist?
this one is supposed to be better; do you think it is?

d) Verbs which are followed by a dass clause or a zu + infinitive very often have an es as object, anticipating the clause or infinitive. There is no equivalent in English:

ich liebe es, alte Filme zu sehen
I love watching old films

ich kann es nicht verstehen, dass er das vergessen hat
I can't understand how he could have forgotten it

See also the use of es *for impersonal verbs (pp 162–64).*

6 The use of pronouns with prepositions

After most prepositions, the third person pronouns (er, sie, es) are usually only used to refer to people:

an sie   **auf ihm**
to her   on him

For a preposition + pronoun referring to an object or idea the form da(r)- + preposition is used:

damit   **dagegen**
with it   against it

There is an -r- when the preposition begins with a vowel: daran, darauf, daraus, darin *etc*:

hast du es daraus genommen?
did you take it out of here?

darin sind wir uns einig   **ich erinnere mich daran**
on that we are agreed   I remember it

This is the case with all prepositions except:

außer	bis	gegenüber
except	until	opposite
ohne	seit	wider
without	since	against

and those taking the genitive:

außerhalb	innerhalb	trotz
outside	within	in spite of
während	wegen	
during	because of	

and others less common.

For the use of the definite article as an alternative to the personal pronouns see pp 19–21.

B REFLEXIVE PRONOUNS

The reflexive pronouns are normally used in the accusative or
dative case. The forms are the same as the accusative and dative
of the personal pronouns except for the third person singular and
second person plural in the 'Sie' form:

PERSON	ACCUSATIVE	DATIVE
ich	mich	mir
du	dich	dir
er	sich	sich
sie	sich	sich
es	sich	sich
wir	uns	uns
ihr	euch	euch
Sie	sich	sich
sie	sich	sich

Note that the reflexive is the only form of the pronoun where the
polite form does not begin with a capital letter.

There is a type of genitive which has the same forms as the genitive
of the personal pronouns. It is used with one or two adjectives,
usually together with **selbst**:

> **sie ist ihrer selbst nicht sicher**
> she's not very sure of herself

For the use of the reflexive see pp 165-67.

C INDEFINITE PRONOUNS

Indefinite pronouns take the place of a noun but do not specify
precisely what they are referring to. Indefinite pronouns are, for
example, 'something', 'everyone'.

1 man (one, you, people, they, we)

a) *forms*

nom	man
acc	einen
dat	einem
There is no genitive form.	
reflexive	sich
possessive	sein

b) *examples:*

heute trägt man keine Hosenträger mehr
people don't wear braces nowadays

man sollte nie sagen, was einem gerade einfällt
you should never say just whatever occurs to you

im Büro hat man mir gesagt ...
they told me in the office ...

2 jemand (anyone, someone, somebody), niemand (no-one, nobody)

nom	jemand	niemand
acc	jemand(en)	niemand(en)
gen	jemandes	niemandes
dat	jemand(em)	niemand(em)

The accusative and dative endings are often left out in spoken German and can be left out in written German.

hat jemand nach mir gefragt?   **ich habe niemand(en) gesehen**
has anyone asked for me?   I saw nobody

The reflexive form of both jemand and niemand is sich; the possessive adjective used with them is sein:

niemand hatte sein Fahrrad dabei
nobody had his/her bicycle with him/her
nobody had their bicycle with them

wenn jemand sich beschwert
if anyone complains

a) jemand and niemand can be combined with sonst (before them) or
anders (after them) to mean 'someone/no-one else':

möchte sonst jemand es probieren?
would someone else like to try?

niemand anders als sein Bruder
none other than his brother

b) jemand can be made even less specific by the addition of irgend:

irgendjemand muss es verloren haben
someone or other must have lost it

komm mit irgendjemand
come with anyone at all

c) jemand and niemand can be combined with adjectival nouns
for phrases of the type of 'somebody interesting' or 'somebody
famous'. Although the adjective can have the -en ending in the
accusative, the following is the commonest form:

nom	jemand Interessantes
acc	jemand Interessantes
dat	jemand Interessantem

Avoid the genitive by using von jemand Interessantem.

3 meinesgleichen (people like me, of my kind):

meinesgleichen does not change its form according to case:

sie redet nicht mit meinesgleichen
she doesn't talk to the likes of me

but forms are possible for all persons: **deinesgleichen, seinesgleichen, unseresgleichen, euresgleichen, Ihresgleichen, ihresgleichen:**

er redet nur mit seinesgleichen
he'll only talk to people on his own level

deinesgleichen kenne ich
I know your sort

ein Werk, das seinesgleichen sucht
a work in a class of its own

4 unsereiner (people of our sort, class)

unsereiner is singular; it can have accusative (**unsereinen**) and dative (**unsereinem**) and feminine forms (**unsereine, unsereine, unsereiner**):

unsereiner kann sich das nicht leisten
our sort can't afford that

unsereinem fehlt das Geld dazu
our sort haven't got the money for it

D UNINFLECTED INDEFINITE PRONOUNS

There is a group of indefinite pronouns which remain the same whatever case they are in:

etwas	**nichts**	**jedermann**
something	nothing	everyone
ein bisschen	**ein paar**	**ein wenig**
a little	a few	a little

ich habe etwas/nichts gehört
I heard something/nothing
nichts war zu hören
nothing was to be heard
mit ein wenig Glück
with a bit of luck

With reflexive verbs they use the reflexive pronoun **sich**; **jedermann** uses the possessive **sein**, whereas **beide** and **ein paar** use **ihr**:

nichts hat sich geändert
nothing has changed

jedermann hat seine Pflicht zu erfüllen
everybody has his duty to do

beide hatten ihre Hausaufgaben nicht gemacht
neither of them had done their homework
both of them had failed to do their homework

1 etwas (something)

es war etwas los
something was going on

hast du etwas gesehen?
have you seen something?

etwas is shortened colloquially to was:

ich werde dir was zeigen
I'll show you something

etwas can be made even less specific by the addition of irgend:

haben Sie irgendetwas gesehen?
did you see anything at all?

irgendwas muss geschehen sein
something must have happened

etwas can be used as an adjective (it still has no endings) before nouns:

etwas Brot
some bread

ich freue mich auf etwas Ruhe
I'm looking forward to some peace and quiet

so etwas is used to mean 'something/anything like that':

hast du je von so etwas gehört?
have you ever heard of anything like it?

so etwas musste kommen
something like that was bound to happen

etwas is used with an + *dat* to translate 'something about':

> **es ist etwas an ihm, was mir nicht gefällt**
> there is something about him I don't like

etwas can be used with an adjectival noun for phrases of the type 'something remarkable' or 'something sad'. The adjective has the neuter endings of adjectives with no article (*see* pp 69-72):

> **das war etwas durchaus Bemerkenswertes**
> that was something quite remarkable

> **die Erinnerung an etwas Trauriges**
> the memory of something sad

> **wir suchen nach etwas Besserem**
> we're looking for something better

2 nichts (nothing, not anything)

> **du hast nichts vergessen?**   **ich habe damit nichts zu tun**
> you've not forgotten anything?   I have nothing to do with it

a) nichts can be intensified by a number of words or phrases to make the equivalent of English 'nothing at all'. All the corresponding German words or phrases come before nichts:

> gar, ganz und gar, rein gar, überhaupt:

> **du hast überhaupt nichts getan!**
> you've done nothing at all

> **ich habe zu gar nichts Lust**
> I don't feel like doing anything at all

b) 'nothing else, other than' is usually translated by sonst nichts:

> **da war sonst nichts zu tun**
> there was nothing else to do

c) nichts ander(e)s als is usually the equivalent of 'nothing other than', though the English translation is often 'could only be described as':

> **das ist nichts ander(e)s als Betrug**
> that can only be described as fraud

d) **nichts** is used with **an** + *dat* for 'nothing about':

nichts an der Sache gefällt dir
you don't like anything about it

e) **nichts** can be used with an adjectival noun for phrases of the
type 'nothing interesting' or 'nothing new'. The adjective has the
endings of the neuter adjective without article (*see* pp 69-72):

nichts Interessantes im Fernsehen?
nothing interesting on TV?

3 ein bisschen (a little), ein paar (a few), ein wenig (a little)

These are all used without any change of form of either part. They
can be used both by themselves as pronouns and before a noun:

ein paar alte Bekannte   **ein paar werden schon kommen**
a few old friends   a few at least will come
ich möchte ein bisschen frische Luft
I'd like a bit of fresh air

4 jedermann (everyone)

jedermann takes a singular verb. It has no endings except for an **-s**
in the genitive:

jedermann hörte den Aufruf
everyone heard the call

das ist nicht jedermanns Sache
that's not everyone's cup of tea

jeder is more common than **jedermann**; *see* p 28.

5 beide (both, the two)

beide sind schon da
both are here

a) beide can also be used after the definite article, a demonstrative
    or a possessive; in such cases it has the endings of an adjective
    after the definite article (*see* **pp 64-6**) whether it is used before a
    noun or by itself:

    die beiden sind gekommen
    the two of them have come

    mit diesen beiden neuen Schülern
    with these two new pupils

    Note the different word order to English:

    die beiden Schüler
    both the pupils

b) The singular beides is a neuter indefinite pronoun which can refer
    back to two objects or ideas but not to people. It is normally only
    used in the nominative (beides), accusative (beides) and dative
    (beidem):

    Hut und Mantel, beides hat er vergessen
    he's forgotten both his hat and coat

    ich bin mit beidem zufrieden   **beides ist teuer**
    I'm happy with either   both are expensive

    beides is used with a singular verb except when sein is followed
    by a plural noun:

    beides bietet Vorteile   **beides ist richtig**
    both have advantages   both are correct

    but: **beides sind Erstaufführungen**
            both are first performances

c) beide is only used in the plural and can refer to both people
    and objects:

nom	beide
acc	beide
gen	beider
dat	beiden

beide wollen kommen
both (of them) want to come

beide waren gleich teuer
both (of them) were just as expensive

d) *Word order:* beide can be used alone before the verb or come later in the sentence when a noun or pronoun is the subject:

beide wollen kommen	**sie wollen beide kommen**
both want to come	they both want to come
die Mädchen wollen beide kommen	**leider kommen beide Mädchen**
the girls both want to come	unfortunately both girls are coming
leider kommen die Mädchen beide	
unfortunately both of the girls are coming	

e) beide can be emphasised by having alle before it:

sind alle beide gekommen?	**ihr seid Schurken, alle beide!**
have both of them come?	you're rascals, the two of you!

f) beide after personal pronouns

The endings of beide can vary when it is used after personal pronouns. In general, beide has the same endings as plural adjectives without an article (*see* pp 69-72):

wir beide	**für euch beide**
both of us	for the two of you
sie beide zusammen	
the two of them together	

except after ihr and between ihr or wir and a noun:

ihr beiden	**ihr beiden Freunde**
both of you	you two friends
wir beiden alten Kumpel	
we two old pals	

Many other types of word can be used as indefinite pronouns:
for the use as indefinite pronouns of the indefinite article, the possessives, derjenige, derselbe, dieser, jeder, keiner, mancher, welcher, alles, alle *(plural) and* solche *(plural) see the individual entries in* Articles pp 25-33

for the use of the interrogative pronoun wer *as an indefinite pronoun see* p 107

for welcher *see* pp 32-3.

E ADJECTIVES USED AS PRONOUNS

1 A number of adjectives can be used without a following noun, ie as a pronoun. They generally have the normal adjective endings according to gender, number, case and whether they are preceded by an article or not:

gestern war ein anderer da
another person was there yesterday

Folgendes muss getan werden
the following must be done

It is often difficult to distinguish these from adjectival nouns.

2 Some adjectives are most commonly used as indefinite pronouns in the plural.

a) einige ('some', 'several'), mehrere ('several'), viele ('much, many') and wenige ('little, few') are the most common:

ich habe einige schon bemerkt	**der Beste unter vielen**
I've noticed several already	the best of many
nur wenige sind erschienen	**er kennt die Arbeiten mehrerer**
only a few turned up	he knows several people's work

b) All (except mehrere) can also be used by themselves as pronouns in the singular, but with certain restrictions.

   i) einiges

   As a singular pronoun, einiges is only used as a neuter collective, not referring to people; its usual English equivalent is 'some things':

einiges, was ihm neu war
some things which were new to him

ich habe einiges mitgebracht
I've brought a few things with me

Like etwas and nichts, it can be used before adjectival nouns:

einiges Interessante
a few interesting things

ii) viel and wenig can have the neuter endings (vieles, vielem):

wir haben viel(es) von ihm gehört
we've heard a lot about him

aus wenig(em) macht er viel(es)   **nur wenig(es) gelang ihm**
he turns a little into a lot   not much turned out right for him

The forms with endings are more common in the dative:

von vielem enttäuscht
disappointed with many things

viel and wenig are very commonly used with adjectival nouns. The more common form is to use viel, wenig without endings whilst the adjectival noun takes the endings of a neuter adjective without an article:

viel Überflüssiges   **neben wenig Ausgezeichnetem**
much that is superfluous   alongside little that was excellent

3 sämtlich ('all without exception') is generally used as a normal adjective but it can be used without an ending and following the verb to emphasise completeness:

sie waren sämtlich erschienen
they all came, every one

F RELATIVE PRONOUNS

The relative pronoun introduces a subordinate clause. It refers back
to a preceding noun, pronoun or clause about which the relative
clause provides further information or definition. For example, in
the sentence, 'the man who did it', 'who' refers back to 'the man'
and the clause 'who did it' tells us more about him.

As these are subordinate clauses, in German the verb goes at the end.

1 Forms

German generally uses the definite article for the relative pronoun.

	MASCULINE	FEMININE	NEUTER	PLURAL ALL GENDERS
nom	der	die	das	die
acc	den	die	das	die
gen	dessen	deren	dessen	deren
dat	dem	der	dem	denen

Note the change in form from the definite article for the genitive
and for the dative plural.

welche is also used as a relative pronoun (*see* p 32-3).

2 Agreement

In English the relative pronouns 'which' and 'that' have only one
form; 'who' has an accusative form 'whom' and a genitive 'whose'.

In German the form varies according to number, gender and case.
The German relative pronoun takes its gender and number from
what it refers back to, but takes its case from its function (subject,
object *etc*) in the relative clause. For example, in the sentence:

der Junge, den ich gestern sah
the boy that I saw yesterday

der Junge is masculine singular; in the relative clause he is what was seen, ie the object; therefore the masculine singular accusative of the relative pronoun is used. *Compare also:*

der Spieler, der gewonnen hat
the player who won

der Betrag, den du zahlen musst
the amount you have to pay

die Lehrer, denen er es erklären muss
the teachers he has to explain it to

die Frau, deren Mann du kennst
the woman whose husband you know

der Mann, dessen Frau du kennst
the man whose wife you know

> ## Note
>
> The relative pronoun can never be omitted in German as it sometimes is in English:
>
> **die Frau, die du kennst**
> the woman you know

3 Use with prepositions

a) Prepositions always come before the relative pronoun, never at the end of the sentence as they sometimes do in English:

die Hausaufgabe, von der du weißt
the homework that you know about

der Zug, mit dem er reist
the train he'll be travelling on

b) When the relative pronoun used with a preposition doesn't refer back to a person but to an object or idea, then the form wo(r) +

preposition is frequently also used. *Compare*:

die Ansagerin, von der er sprach
the announcer he spoke about

and:

das Thema, worüber er sprach
das Thema, über das er sprach
the subject he spoke about

The form **wor-** is used with prepositions that begin with a vowel.

4 The alternative neuter form was

was is normally used for the neuter nominative and accusative to refer back to the following:

a) *indefinite neuter pronouns* such as alles, etwas, nichts (*for list see above*):

nichts, was mich interessierte
nothing that I was interested in

etwas, was mir Sorgen machte
something that worried me

einiges, was ich bedenken sollte
some things I should consider

When das is used instead of **was**, especially after etwas, it is because the speaker has something specific in mind. *Compare*:

gibt es irgendetwas, was ich tun kann?
is there anything I can do?

and:

er sah etwas, das ihn schockierte
he saw something that shocked me

b) *a neuter adjectival noun:*

das Beste, was du tun kannst
the best you can do

das meiste, was ich gelesen habe
the most that I have read

c) *a whole clause:*

er sagte ab, was alle bedauerten
he cancelled, which everyone regretted

die Regierung trat zurück, was Neuwahlen erforderlich machte
the government resigned, which led to a general election

Note that was is not used with a preposition:

er rutschte aus, worüber alle lachten
he slipped, which made everyone laugh

5 Replacement of the relative pronoun by wo (where)

a) Clauses of place are often introduced by the conjunction wo ('where') instead of the preposition + relative pronoun:

ein Land, wo er viel Zeit verbrachte
a country in which he spent a lot of time

b) When the relative refers back to the name of a country, town or place, wo must be used instead of a preposition + relative pronoun:

Rom, wo es so viele schöne Kirchen gibt
Rome, where there are so many fine churches

c) wo is also often used in place of a preposition + relative pronoun in clauses of time:

die Jahre, wo er viel verdiente
the years in which he earned a lot

die Woche, wo ich verreist war
the week in which I was away

6 wer as a relative pronoun

The interrogatives wer and was (*for forms see below*) can each be used as relative pronouns without implying a question, when the relative clause starts a sentence and is the subject of the main verb. The English equivalent is usually 'anyone who' or 'whoever':

wer das kauft, muss schwachsinnig sein
whoever buys that must be daft

wer wagt, gewinnt
he who dares wins

wem der Mut fehlt, darf gehen
anyone who lacks the courage may go

G INTERROGATIVE PRONOUNS

1 There are two interrogative pronouns, one for persons (wer) and one for things (was):

	PERSONAL	IMPERSONAL
nom	wer	was
acc	wen	was
gen	wessen	wessen
dat	wem	-

wer kommt heute?
who's coming today?

wessen Mantel ist das?
whose coat is that?

auf wen kann ich rechnen?
who can I count on?

was sagst du?
what do you say?

mit wem geht sie aus?
who is she going out with?

2 They are all usually singular, but take a plural of the verb sein if followed by a plural noun:

wer sind deine Begleiter?
who are your companions?

was sind seine Gründe?
what are his reasons?

3 Use with prepositions

When used with a preposition, was is replaced by the wo(r) + preposition forms of the relative pronoun:

womit soll ich es waschen?
what shall I wash it with?

woran liegt das?
what's the cause of it?

4 When the clause introduced by the interrogative pronoun follows a verb of saying, asking or similar, it is a subordinate clause (an indirect question) and the verb therefore goes to the end:

weißt du, wer heute kommt?
do you know who's coming today?

erzähl mir, was er gesagt hat
tell me what he said

For the alternative use of welcher? *as an interrogative pronoun see pp 32-3.*

 H THE ORDER OF PRONOUNS

For a fuller treatment see pp 236-39.

1 Pronouns as direct and indirect objects generally come immediately after the verb:

ich gebe dir das Geld
I'll give you the money

ich habe ihm das Buch geliehen
I lent him the book

a) When there are two pronoun objects the accusative one comes before the dative:

habe ich es dir gegeben?
did I give it to you?

ich habe es ihm geliehen
I lent it to him

b) The same order applies when one is a dative reflexive pronoun:

ich kann es mir nicht leisten
I can't afford it

c) Otherwise the reflexive pronoun generally comes immediately after the verb:

er kauft sich einen Filzstift
he's buying a felt-tip pen

2 A pronoun subject must come immediately after the verb when there is an inversion:

morgens macht sie ihm das Frühstück
in the mornings she makes his breakfast for him

gestern hat sie ihn gesehen
she saw him yesterday

3 A noun subject can come before or after a pronoun object:

gestern hat ihn meine Schwester gesehen
gestern hat meine Schwester ihn gesehen
my sister saw him yesterday

7 VERBS

The section on verbs is divided into the following:

    A. Verb types and forms

    B. Notes on verb forms

    C. Use of tenses

    D. Conjugation tables

A VERB TYPES AND FORMS

1 Types of verbs

There are two main types of verb in German, generally referred to as weak and strong verbs. Weak verbs conform to a group pattern with a few standard variations. Strong verbs have a common basic pattern but a much greater degree of variation within it so that the main parts have to be learnt for each individual verb. There is a small number of verbs of mixed type. *For a list of the main parts of strong and mixed verbs, see pp 120-27 and 131-34.*

The fundamental difference between the two types is in the formation of the imperfect tense and the past participle: the weak verbs add a characteristic -t- to the verb stem (= infinitive without -(e)n ending) in these forms; strong verbs change the stem vowel of the infinitive when forming the imperfect tense and past participle, for example:

		IMPERFECT	PAST PARTICIPLE
weak:	packen	ich packte	gepackt
strong:	singen	ich sang	gesungen

These two basic types are similar to the two basic verb types in English (from the example above, English pack - packed - packed and sing - sang - sung). This similarity of verb form between English and German is very helpful in learning German verbs - but it does not always apply. However, if an English and German verb have the same root (eg packen - to pack, singen - to sing, sagen - to say, lieben - to love) the likelihood is that they will both be of the same type. Exceptions such as helfen (strong) and 'to help' (weak) should act as a warning to check if in doubt.

By far the largest number of verbs belong to the weak group. New creations are always weak (eg managen - gemanagt) and some verbs which were originally strong are gradually adopting weak forms (eg for the verb stecken ['to be in a situation'] in the imperfect tense the strong form stak is often replaced by the weak form steckte). Many strong verbs, however, are very common verbs, eg sein ('to be'), gehen ('to go') *etc.*

2 Tenses, moods and voices

a) *main tenses:*

   i) present

   ii) imperfect

   iii) perfect

   iv) pluperfect

   v) future

   vi) future perfect

b) *moods:*

   i) indicative

   ii) imperative

   iii) subjunctive

   iv) conditional

c) *voices:*

    i) active

    ii) passive

d) *the infinitive:*

The form in which the verb is usually given in dictionaries is called the infinitive. It consists of the verb stem plus (e)n. It is the equivalent of the English form with 'to': to read = lesen (les + en).

3 Verb forms: the conjugation of verbs

a) *weak verbs*

    i) Present tense

The present tense is formed by adding the endings -e, -st, -t, -en, -t, -en to the stem.

infinitive	fragen	reden	heizen
ich	frage	rede	heize
du	fragst	redest	heizt
er/sie/es	fragt	redet	heizt
wir	fragen	reden	heizen
ihr	fragt	redet	heizt
Sie/sie	fragen	reden	heizen

infinitive	atmen	klingeln	plaudern
ich	atme	klingle	plaud(e)re
du	atmest	kingelst	plauderst
er/sie/es	atmet	klingelt	plaudert
wir	atmen	klingeln	plaudern
ihr	atmet	klingelt	plaudert
Sie/sie	atmen	klingeln	plaudern

haben is a weak verb but has slightly irregular forms:

ich	**habe**
du	**hast**

er/sie/es	hat
wir	haben
ihr	habt
Sie/sie	haben

Standard variations:

An -e- is inserted before the -st and -t endings for verbs whose stem ends in -t or -d (*see* reden *above*). This is also the case with verbs whose stem ends in an -m or -n (but not -mm, -nn, -lm, -ln, -rm or -rn): *see* atmen *above*; filmen ('to film') would not need the extra -e-.

In verbs whose stem ends in -s, -ß, -x, -z the s of the -st ending is omitted (*see* heizen *above*).

Verbs whose infinitive ends in -eln lose the e before the l in the ich form (*see* klingeln *above*); this can also happen in verbs ending in -ern but is not obligatory (*see* plaudern *above*).

ii) Imperfect tense

The imperfect tense is formed by adding the endings -te, -test, -te, -ten, -tet, -ten to the stem.

infinitive	fragen	reden	atmen
ich	fragte	redete	atmete
du	fragtest	redetest	atmetest
er/sie/es	fragte	redete	atmete
wir	fragten	redeten	atmeten
ihr	fragtet	redetet	atmetet
Sie/sie	fragten	redeten	atmeten

haben loses the -b- of the stem in the imperfect tense:

ich	hatte
du	hattest
er/sie/es	hatte
wir	hatten
ihr	hattet
Sie/sie	hatten

Standard variations:

In verbs whose stems end in -d or -t, or in -m or -n (but not -mm, -nn, -lm, -ln, -rm or -rn): an e is inserted between the stem and the ending (*see* reden, atmen *above*).

iii) Perfect tense

The perfect tense is formed by using the past participle (*for the formation of the past participle see* **section xiv** *below*) with the present tense of sein or haben. *For the question of whether to use* sein *or* haben *see* pp 134–37 *below.*

fragen		reisen	
ich habe..............	gefragt	ich bin..............	gereist
du hast..............	gefragt	du bist..............	gereist
er/sie/es hat.......	gefragt	er/sie/es ist.....	gereist
wir haben..............	gefragt	wir sind.............	gereist
ihr habt..............	gefragt	ihr seid.............	gereist
Sie/sie haben.....	gefragt	Sie/sie sind......	gereist

The participle normally comes at the end of the sentence or clause.

iv) Pluperfect tense

The pluperfect is formed by using the past participle (*for the formation of the past participle see* **section xiv** *below*) together with the imperfect tense of sein or haben. *For the question of whether to use* sein *or* haben *see* pp 134–37 *below.*

fragen		reisen	
ich hatte..............	gefragt	ich war..............	gereist
du hattest..............	gefragt	du warst.............	gereist
er/sie/es hatte....	gefragt	er/sie/es war...	gereist
wir hatten.............	gefragt	wir waren..........	gereist
ihr hattet..............	gefragt	ihr wart.............	gereist
Sie/sie hatten.....	gefragt	Sie/sie waren..	gereist

The participle normally comes at the end of the sentence or clause.

v) Future tense

The future is formed by using the present tense of werden plus the infinitive:

fragen
ich werde............ fragen
du wirst............... fragen
er/sie/es wird.... fragen
wir werden......... fragen
ihr werdet........... fragen
Sie/sie werden.. fragen

The infinitive normally comes at the end of the sentence or clause.

vi) Future perfect

The future perfect is formed by using the present tense of werden plus the perfect infinitive (*see* **section xv** *below*). *For the question of whether to use sein or haben see* **pp 134-7** below:

fragen		reisen	
ich werde...........	gefragt haben	ich werde..........	gereist sein
du wirst..............	gefragt haben	du wirst.............	gereist sein
er/sie/es wird...	gefragt haben	er/sie/es wird..	gereist sein
wir werden........	gefragt haben	wir werden.......	gereist sein
ihr werdet..........	gefragt haben	ihr werdet.........	gereist sein
Sie/sie werden.	gefragt haben	Sie/sie werden.	gereist sein

vii) Imperative (*for usage and alternative forms see* **p 146** *below*).

There are imperatives for the du, ihr, Sie and wir forms of the verb. The imperative of the du form is the stem of the verb to which an -e is sometimes added; the others have the same endings as in the indicative. The du and ihr forms are normally used without a pronoun, the Sie and wir forms retain the pronoun but with inversion.

It is usual in German to have an exclamation mark at the end of an imperative.

fragen	entschuldigen	klingeln
frag(e)!	entschuldige!	klingle!
fragen wir!	entschuldigen wir!	klingeln wir!
fragt!	entschuldigt!	klingelt!
fragen Sie!	entschuldigen Sie!	klingeln Sie!

The -e- of the second person singular is normally left off, especially in spoken language; it is quite correct to omit it in written German. It is retained for verbs ending in -igen (see entschuldigen above).

Those verbs ending in -eln, -ern normally omit the e of the stem and retain the final -e (see klingeln above).

Verbs whose stems end in two different consonants retain the -e for reasons of ease of pronunciation (eg atme!, antworte!); verbs with a stem ending in -d or -t often keep the -e (red! or rede!, bet! or bete!).

viii) Present subjunctive

The present subjunctive is formed by adding the following endings to the verb stem: -e, -est, -e, -en, -et, -en.

fragen	haben
ich frage	ich habe
du fragest	du habest
er/sie/es frage	er/sie/es habe
wir fragen	wir haben
ihr fraget	ihr habet
Sie/sie fragen	Sie/sie haben

haben is regular in the present subjunctive.

ix) Imperfect subjunctive

The imperfect subjunctive for weak verbs is the same as the imperfect indicative (see **section ii** above).

haben has an umlaut in the imperfect subjunctive:

ich hätte
du hättest
er/sie/es hätte
wir hätten
ihr hättet
Sie/sie hätten

x) Perfect and pluperfect subjunctives

The perfect and pluperfect subjunctives are formed in the
same way as the perfect and pluperfect tenses in the indicative
except that the present or imperfect subjunctive of sein or
haben is substituted for the present or imperfect indicative.

fragen		reisen	
ich habe/hätte..............	gefragt	ich sei/wäre....................	gereist
du habest/hättest.........	gefragt	du sei(e)st/wär(e)st.........	gereist
er/sie/es habe/hätte....	gefragt	er/sie/es sei/wäre...........	gereist
wir haben/hätten.........	gefragt	wir seien/wären..............	gereist
ihr habet/hättet............	gefragt	ihr seiet/wär(e)t..............	gereist
Sie/sie haben/hätten....	gefragt	Sie/sie seien/wären........	gereist

xi) Conditional: the subjunctive formed with würde

Very often the standard present, imperfect and perfect subjunctives
are replaced by a compound form using the imperfect subjunctive
of werden plus the infinitive or the perfect infinitive:

fragen
ich würde...................... fragen
du würdest.................... fragen
er/sie/es würde............ fragen
wir würden................... fragen
ihr würdet..................... fragen
Sie/sie würden.............. fragen

ich würde...................... gefragt haben
du würdest.................... gefragt haben

er/sie/es würde.............	gefragt haben
wir würden......................	gefragt haben
ihr würdet.......................	gefragt haben
Sie/sie würden..............	gefragt haben

xii) Passives

There are two forms of the passive in German, one using the auxiliary werden, the other using sein. Both use the past participle of the verb. For a distinction of the usage see **pp 144–45** below.

passive with werden		*passive with* sein	
ich werde......................	gefragt	ich bin......................	gefragt
du wirst......................	gefragt	du bist......................	gefragt
er/sie/es wird..............	gefragt	er/sie/es ist..............	gefragt
wir werden......................	gefragt	wir sind......................	gefragt
ihr werdet......................	gefragt	ihr seid......................	gefragt
Sie/sie werden..............	gefragt	Sie/sie sind..............	gefragt

More complex tenses can be formed by using the other tenses of werden with the past participle:

imperfect passive:
ich wurde...   **gefragt** *etc*

perfect passive:
ich bin...   **gefragt worden** *etc*

Note the special form of the past participle of werden used to form the passive.

pluperfect passive:
ich war...   **gefragt worden** *etc*

future passive:
ich werde...   **gefragt werden** *etc*

future perfect passive:
ich werde...   **gefragt worden sein** *etc*

Passive subjunctives can also be formed by using the subjunctive of werden.

xiii) Present participle

The present participle is formed by adding -d to the infinitive. *For usage see* pp 155–56.

xiv) Past participle

The past participle is formed from the verb stem plus (e)t and normally begins with the prefix ge-:

gefragt	geatmet	geheizt	geredet

The final t is preceded by an e in verbs whose stems end in -d or -t or in a consonant preceded by a different consonant except for l or r.

In separable verbs the ge- is placed between the separable prefix and the verb stem, eg ausgefragt, zurückgereist, eingeatmet.

The prefix ge- is omitted in verbs with an inseparable prefix and verbs ending in -ieren:

besucht	verletzt	übernachtet
erwartet	vollendet	telefoniert

This also includes separable verbs ending in -ieren or those comprised of a separable prefix attached to a verb which already has an inseparable prefix:

einstudiert	anerkannt

Verbs which can be separable or inseparable (*see* p 140) can have two past participles:

übersetzt	translated	übergesetzt	ferried over

xv) Infinitive

The infinitive is the basic form of the verb as it appears in dictionaries *etc.* It always ends in -(e)n and does not change its form, but different tenses of the infinitive can be created by combining it with auxiliary verbs:

infinitive	**sehen** (to see)
perfect infinitive	**gesehen haben** (to have seen)
passive infinitive	**gesehen werden** (to be seen)
passive infinitive	**gesehen sein** (to be seen)
perfect infinitive passive	**gesehen worden sein** (to have been seen)

b) *strong verbs*

   i) Present tense

The present tense is formed by adding the endings -e, -(e)st, -(e)t, -en, -(e)t, -en to the verb stem. In some verbs the vowel of the stem changes in the second and third person singular.

infinitive	**finden**	**sehen**	**fahren**
ich	**finde**	**sehe**	**fahre**
du	**findest**	**siehst**	**fährst**
er/sie/es	**findet**	**sieht**	**fährt**
wir	**finden**	**sehen**	**fahren**
ihr	**findet**	**seht**	**fahrt**
Sie/sie	**finden**	**sehen**	**fahren**

infinitive	**stoßen**	**gehen**	**werfen**
ich	**stoße**	**gehe**	**werfe**
du	**stößt**	**gehst**	**wirfst**
er/sie/es	**stößt**	**geht**	**wirft**
wir	**stoßen**	**gehen**	**werfen**
ihr	**stoßt**	**geht**	**werft**
Sie/sie	**stoßen**	**gehen**	**werfen**

infinitive	**sein**	**werden**	**bitten**
ich	**bin**	**werde**	**bitte**
du	**bist**	**wirst**	**bittest**
er/sie/es	**ist**	**wird**	**bittet**
wir	**sind**	**werden**	**bitten**
ihr	**seid**	**werdet**	**bittet**
Sie/sie	**sind**	**werden**	**bitten**

Note that **sein** is completely irregular in the present tense.

The extra -e- is added to the **du, er/sie/es** and **ihr** forms for verbs whose stems end in -d or -t, except when there has been a vowel change. Compare **finden, bitten** above with:

laden	**lädst**	**raten**	**rätst**	**schelten**	**schiltst**
schmelzen	**schmilzt**	**treten**	**trittst**		

The commonest changes of stem vowels in the **du** and **er/sie/es** forms are:

a → ä: *see* **fahren** *above*. Almost all strong verbs with **a** as a stem vowel modify it to **ä**, except **schaffen**; **backen** is nowadays commonly found without an umlaut and with a weak imperfect tense.

e (short) → i: *see* **werden, werfen** *above*. Most verbs with **e (short)** as a stem vowel modify it to **i**.

e (long) → ie: *see* **sehen** *above*. This is most common when **e** is followed by **h**:

befehlen	**befiehlt**	**gebären**	**gebiert**
geschehen	**geschieht**	**lesen**	**liest**

ii) Imperfect tense

Most strong verbs change the stem vowel for the imperfect tense; there is no ending added for the **ich** and **er/sie/es** forms; all the other forms have the same endings as the present tense.

infinitive	pfeifen	finden	bleiben
ich	pfiff	fand	blieb
du	pfiffst	fandst	bliebst
er/sie/es	pfiff	fand	blieb
wir	pfiffen	fanden	blieben
ihr	pfifft	fandet	bliebt
Sie/sie	pfiffen	fanden	blieben
infinitive	schließen	helfen	sein
ich	schloss	half	war
du	schlossest	halfst	warst
er/sie/es	schloss	half	war

wir	schlossen	halfen	waren
ihr	schlosst	halft	wart
Sie/sie	schlossen	halfen	waren

In the imperfect tense the -e- inserted after verb stems that end in -d, -t *etc* is felt to be particularly stilted. It is almost never inserted in spoken German and is normally avoided in written German except for the du forms of verbs whose stems end in -s, -sch, -x, -z (*see* schließen *above*) and for the ihr forms of verbs with stems ending in -d and -t (*see* finden *above*).

For a list of strong verbs in the imperfect, see **pp 173–78**.

Some verbs have a change in the final consonant of the stem, eg ziehen → ich zog. *See the list on* **pp 173–78**.

werden has an irregular imperfect tense as it changes the vowel but adds the weak endings (the older, strong form – ich ward, du ward(e)st, er ward in the singular – will occasionally be met in older literary works):

ich wurde
du wurdest
er/sie/es wurde
wir wurden
ihr wurdet
Sie/sie wurden

iii) Perfect tense

The perfect tense is formed by using the past participle (*for the formation of the past participle see* **section xiv**) with the present tense of sein or haben. *For the question of whether to use* sein *or* haben *see* **pp 134–37**:

fahren		finden	
ich bin.............	gefahren	ich habe...........	gefunden
du bist.............	gefahren	du hast.............	gefunden
er/sie/es ist...	gefahren	er/sie/es hat...	gefunden

wir sind............	gefahren	wir haben..........	gefunden
ihr seid..............	gefahren	ihr habt.............	gefunden
Sie/sie sind.....	gefahren	Sie/sie haben...	gefunden

The participle normally comes at the end of the sentence or clause.

iv) Pluperfect tense

The pluperfect tense is formed by using the past participle (*for the formation of the past participle see* section xiv *below*) with the imperfect tense of sein or haben. *For the question of whether to use* sein *or* haben *see* pp 134–37 *below*.

fahren		finden	
ich war.............	gefahren	ich hatte............	gefunden
du warst............	gefahren	du hattest.........	gefunden
er/sie/es war...	gefahren	er/sie/es hatte.	gefunden
wir waren.........	gefahren	wir hatten.........	gefunden
ihr wart.............	gefahren	ihr hattet..........	gefunden
Sie/sie waren..	gefahren	Sie/sie hatten..	gefunden

The past participle normally comes at the end of the sentence or clause.

v) Future tense

The future tense is formed by using the infinitive with the present tense of werden:

fahren	
ich werde..........	fahren
du wirst.............	fahren
er/sie/es wird..	fahren
wir werden.......	fahren
ihr werdet.........	fahren
Sie/sie werden.	fahren

The infinitive normally comes at the end of the sentence or clause.

vi) Future perfect

The future perfect is formed by using the perfect infinitive (ie the past participle with the infinitive of **sein** or **haben**) with the present tense of **werden**. For the question of whether to use **sein** or **haben** *see* pp 134–37.

fahren		finden	
ich werde..........	gefahren sein	ich werde..........	gefunden haben
du wirst..............	gefahren sein	du wirst..............	gefunden haben
er/sie/es wird..	gefahren sein	er/sie/es wird..	gefunden haben
wir werden.......	gefahren sein	wir werden........	gefunden haben
ihr werdet.........	gefahren sein	ihr werdet.........	gefunden haben
Sie/sie werden.	gefahren sein	Sie/sie werden.	gefunden haben

vii) Imperative (*for usage and alternative forms see* p 146)

The imperative is used with the **du**, **ihr**, **Sie** and **wir** forms of the verb alone. The **du** form is the stem of the verb to which an -e is sometimes added; the others have the same endings as in the indicative. The **du** and **ihr** forms are normally used without a pronoun, the **Sie** and **wir** forms retain the pronoun but with inversion.

It is usual in German to have an exclamation mark at the end of an imperative.

fahren
fahr(e)!
fahren wir!
fahrt!
fahren Sie!

The -e ending of the **du** form is normally left off, especially in spoken German; it is quite correct to omit it in written German.

Verbs which change the stem vowel from **e** to **i** in the **du** form of the indicative also have the change in the imperative:

sehen
sieh(e)!

sehen wir!
seht!
sehen Sie!

but:

Verbs which change from a to ä do not have the change in the imperative (*see* fahren *above*).

Note that the du form of the imperative of werden is werde!

The imperative of sein:

sei!
seien wir!
seid!
seien Sie!

viii) Present subjunctive

The present subjunctive is formed by adding the following endings to the stem: -e, -est, -e, -en, -et, -en. No verbs change the stem vowel.

infinitive	fahren	sehen
ich	fahre	sehe
du	fahrest	sehest
er/sie/es	fahre	sehe
wir	fahren	sehen
ihr	fahret	sehet
Sie/sie	fahren	sehen

ix) Imperfect subjunctive

The imperfect subjunctive is formed by adding the endings -e, -est, -e, -en, -et, -en to the stem of the imperfect tense. If the vowel of the stem is a, o or u it always has an umlaut.

fahren	bleiben	sein
ich führe	ich bliebe	ich wäre
du führest	du bliebest	du wär(e)st
er/sie/es führe	er/sie/es bliebe	er/sie/es wäre
wir führen	wir blieben	wir wären
ihr führet	ihr bliebet	ihr wär(e)t
Sie/sie führen	Sie/sie blieben	Sie/sie wären

x) Perfect and pluperfect subjunctives

The perfect and pluperfect subjunctives are formed in the same way as the perfect and pluperfect indicatives (*see* **sections iii and iv** *above*) except that the present or imperfect subjunctive of sein or haben is substituted for the present or imperfect indicative.

fahren		finden	
ich sei/wäre....	gefahren	ich habe/hätte..	gefunden
du sei(e)st/ wär(e)st..........	gefahren	du habest/ hättest.............	gefunden
er/sie/es sei/ wäre................	gefahren	er/sie/es habe/ hätte................	gefunden
wir seien/ wären..............	gefahren	wir haben/ hätten..............	gefunden
ihr seiet/ wär(e)t............	gefahren	ihr habet/ hättet.............	gefunden
Sie/sie seien/ wären..............	gefahren	Sie/sie haben/ hätten.............	gefunden

xi) Conditionals or subjunctives with würde

As for weak verbs. *See* **section a) xi** *above*.

xii) Passives

As for weak verbs. *See* **section a) xii** *above*.

xiii) Present participle

As for weak verbs. *See* **section a) xiii** *above*.

xiv) Past participle

The past participle is formed from the verb stem (usually with a change of vowel) which is normally preceded by the prefix ge- and followed by -en:

fahren	gefahren	bleiben	geblieben
werfen	geworfen	singen	gesungen

The past participle of sein is **gewesen**

In separable verbs the ge- is placed between the prefix and the verb stem:

einschlafen   eingeschlafen   **aussteigen**   ausgestiegen

The ge- is omitted in verbs that have an inseparable prefix:

verstehen   verstanden   **empfehlen**   empfohlen

c) *modal verbs*

  i) Present tense

    The present tense has no endings on the verb stem in the ich and er/sie/es forms; the ending for du is -st, those for wir, ihr and Sie/sie are -en, -t, -en. The vowel of the verb stem in the singular is different from that of the infinitive and plural forms, except for sollen.

infinitive	dürfen	können	mögen
ich	darf	kann	mag
du	darfst	kannst	magst
er/sie/es	darf	kann	mag
wir	dürfen	können	mögen
ihr	dürft	könnt	mögt
Sie/sie	dürfen	können	mögen

infinitive	müssen	sollen	wollen
ich	muss	soll	will
du	musst	sollst	willst
er/sie/es	muss	soll	will
wir	müssen	sollen	wollen
ihr	müsst	sollt	wollt
Sie/sie	müssen	sollen	wollen

  ii) Imperfect tense

    The imperfect tense is formed with the same endings as weak verbs (*see* **pp 113–14**) but there is a change of stem vowel, except for sollen and wollen.

infinitive	dürfen	können	mögen
ich	durfte	konnte	mochte
du	durftest	konntest	mochtest
er/sie/es	durfte	konnte	mochte

wir	durften	konnten	mochten
ihr	durftet	konntet	mochtet
Sie/sie	durften	konnten	mochten
infinitive	müssen	sollen	wollen
ich	musste	sollte	wollte
du	musstest	solltest	wolltest
er/sie/es	musste	sollte	wollte
wir	mussten	sollten	wollten
ihr	musstet	solltet	wolltet
Sie/sie	mussten	sollten	wollten

Note the change of consonant in mögen.

iii) Perfect and pluperfect tenses

The perfect and pluperfect tenses are formed using haben. When the six modal verbs are used in their commonest function as auxiliary verbs the infinitive is used instead of the past participle:

ich habe/hatte...............	gehen dürfen
du hast/hattest.............	gehen dürfen
er/sie/es hat/hatte......	gehen dürfen
wir haben/hatten..........	gehen dürfen
ihr habt/hattet...............	gehen dürfen
Sie/sie haben/hatten...	gehen dürfen

The modal verbs also have a regular past participle formed in the same way as those of weak verbs except that those that have an umlaut lose it:

gedurft   gekonnt   gemocht   gemusst   gesollt   gewollt

There is another form of the perfect tense using the present indicative of the modal verbs with the perfect infinitive of the verb, that is the past participle plus the infinitive of sein or haben:

ich kann.........	gesehen haben	ich muss..........	gefahren sein
du kannst.......	gesehen haben	du musst..........	gefahren sein

etc

For the distinction in sense between these two forms *see* pp 161–62.

iv) Future tense

The future tense is formed by the present tense of werden combined with the infinitive of the main verb and the infinitive of the modal verb:

ich werde............ kommen können
du wirst.............. kommen können
er/sie/es wird.... kommen können
wir werden......... kommen können
ihr werdet........... kommen können
Sie/sie werden... kommen können

v) Future Perfect

The future perfect is formed by the present tense of werden plus the perfect infinitive of the main verb and the infinitive of the modal verb. This clumsy form is almost never used. A sentence such as:

sie glaubt nicht, dass ich es bis morgen werde geschrieben haben können

is less common than the equivalent English form:

she doesn't think I will have been able to write it by tomorrow

The simpler form:

sie glaubt nicht, dass ich es bis morgen geschrieben habe

expresses practically the same idea.

vi) Present subjunctive

The present subjunctive is formed by adding the following endings to the infinitive stem: -e, -est, -e, -en, -et, -en.

ich könne
du könnest
er/sie/es könne
wir können
ihr könnet
Sie/sie können

vii) Imperfect subjunctive

The imperfect subjunctive is the same as the imperfect indicative, except that those modal verbs which have an umlaut on the stem vowel in the infinitive also have it in the imperfect subjunctive:

ich	könnte	möchte	wollte
du	könntest	möchtest	wolltest
er/sie/es	könnte	möchte	wollte
wir	könnten	möchten	wollten
ihr	könntet	möchtet	wolltet
Sie/sie	könnten	möchten	wollten

Note the change of consonant in mögen

viii) Perfect subjunctive

There are two forms of the perfect subjunctive.

One is formed with the present subjunctive of haben combined with the infinitive of the main verb and the infinitive of the modal verb:

ich habe............ sehen können
du habest........... sehen können
er/sie/es habe.. sehen können
wir haben........... sehen können
ihr habet............ sehen können
Sie/sie haben... sehen können

The other is formed by using the present subjunctive of the modal verb with the perfect infinitive of the main verb:

ich könne.......... gesehen haben		ich müsse........... gefahren sein
du könnest........ gesehen haben		du müssest........ gefahren sein
er/sie/es könne............	gesehen haben	er/sie/es müsse............	gefahren sein
wir können....... gesehen haben		wir müssen........ gefahren sein
ihr könnet......... gesehen haben		ihr müsset.......... gefahren sein
Sie/sie können.. gesehen haben		Sie/sie müssen.. gefahren sein

ix) Pluperfect subjunctive

There are two forms of the pluperfect subjunctive.

One is formed with the imperfect subjunctive of haben combined with the infinitive of the main verb and the infinitive of the modal verb:

ich hätte...........	sehen können
du hättest.........	sehen können
er/sie/es hätte.	sehen können
wir hätten.........	sehen können
ihr hättet..........	sehen können
Sie/sie hätten..	sehen können

The other is formed by using the imperfect subjunctive of the modal with the past infinitive of the main verb (*see* p 119–20):

ich könnte.........	gesehen haben	ich müsste.............	gefahren sein
du könntest......	gesehen haben	du müsstest.........	gefahren sein
er/sie/es könnte............	gesehen haben	er/sie/es müsste..	gefahren sein
wir könnten......	gesehen haben	wir müssten..........	gefahren sein
ihr könntet........	gesehen haben	ihr müsstet............	gefahren sein
Sie/sie könnten..........	gesehen haben	Sie/sie müssten....	gefahren sein

d) *verbs of mixed type*

i) A group of verbs has the endings of the weak conjugation but changes the stem vowel from -e- in the infinitive and present to -a- in the imperfect tense and past participle. Apart from this vowel change, they are perfectly regular weak verbs. They are: brennen, kennen, nennen, rennen:

infinitive	*present*	*imperfect*	*past participle*
brennen	ich brenne	ich brannte	gebrannt
kennen	ich kenne	ich kannte	gekannt

etc

The imperfect subjunctive is also irregular:

ich brennte   **ich kennte**

etc

ii) Two verbs which can conjugate in this way can also have a
regular weak imperfect and past participle:

infinitive	*present*	*imperfect*	*past participle*
senden	ich sende	ich sandte	gesandt
	etc	ich sendete	gesendet
wenden	ich wende	ich wandte	gewandt
	etc	ich wendete	gewendet

They have only one imperfect subjunctive form which is the
same as the regular weak imperfect indicative.

Note the difference in meaning for **senden**:

senden	(regular weak verb)	= to broadcast
	(mixed verb)	= to send

Both forms can be used for most meanings of **wenden**; the form
with the vowel change being slightly more literary. **wenden**
meaning 'to turn' in sewing must have the regular forms.

iii) **denken** and **bringen** change both the vowel and final consonant
of the stem in the imperfect and past participle but have
regular weak endings eg:

infinitive	present	imperfect	past participle
bringen	ich bringe	ich brachte	gebracht
denken	ich denke	ich dachte	gedacht *etc*

The imperfect subjunctive is:

ich brächte   **ich dächte**   *etc*

iv) **wissen**
   wissen forms its main tenses in a similar way to the modal verbs:

present	ich weiß
	du weißt
	er/sie/es weiß
	wir wissen
	ihr wisst
	Sie/sie wissen

imperfect	ich wusste
	du wusstest
	er/sie/es wusste
	wir wussten
	ihr wusstet
	Sie/sie wussten

| *past participle* | gewusst |

present subjunctive	ich wisse
	du wissest
	er/sie/es wisse
	wir wissen
	ihr wisset
	Sie/sie wissen

imperfect subjunctive	ich wüsste
	du wüsstest
	er/sie/es wüsste
	wir wüssten
	ihr wüsstet
	Sie/sie wüssten

v) A small number of verbs have parallel weak and strong forms, sometimes with a difference in sense between the two forms.

Many are not commonly needed for everyday use but two more common examples are noted here:

bewegen (bewegte, bewegt)	= to move
bewegen (bewog, bewogen)	= to persuade someone (to do something)
schaffen (schaffte, geschafft)	= to do, achieve
schaffen (schuf, geschaffen)	= to create

vi) some verbs have a combination of strong and weak forms:

| mahlen | mahlte | gemahlen |
| salzen | salzte | gesalzen |

In some cases a more modern weak form is replacing an older strong one:

backen - backte *(older:* buk*)* - gebacken

 B NOTES ON VERB FORMS

1 The formation of compound tenses with haben or sein

a) haben *is used*

i) with all transitive verbs, ie verbs that can take an object:

er hat die Wurst gegessen
he ate the sausage

This applies even where the verb is used without an object:

er hat schon gegessen
he has already eaten

The few exceptions are transitive verbs formed by adding a prefix to a verb that normally takes **sein**:

er ist seinen Husten noch nicht losgeworden
he hasn't got rid of his cough yet

ii) with intransitive verbs denoting activity:

du hast aber fleißig gearbeitet
you have been working hard

iii) with all reflexive verbs:

hast du dich schon gewaschen?
have you washed yet?

iv) with modal verbs:

mein Sohn hat den Film nicht sehen können
my son couldn't see the film

das habe ich nicht gewollt
that wasn't my intention

solche Musik habe ich immer gemocht
I've always liked that kind of music

v) with impersonal verbs:

es hat geregnet
it rained

except:

gelingen	**misslingen**	**glücken**	**missglücken**
geschehen	**passieren**	**vorkommen**	**widerfahren**

es ist ihm gelungen   **es ist schon passiert, dass ...**
he succeeded   it's happened before that ...

except impersonal expressions with verbs that normally take sein:

wie ist es dir ergangen?
how did you get on?

b) sein *is used*

i) with intransitive verbs expressing change of place, state or situation. The most frequently used verbs of this type are those expressing motion from one place to another:

er ist nach Hause gegangen   **das Geld ist verschwunden**
he has gone home   the money's disappeared
das Haus ist abgebrannt
the house has burnt down

    ii) with the verbs listed as exceptions of v above, whether used impersonally or not:

        der Plan ist missglückt
        the plan failed

    iii) with **sein** and **werden** used both as auxiliary verbs and as full verbs:

        das wäre besser gewesen   **die Milch ist sauer geworden**
        that would have been better   the milk has gone off

        der Vorschlag ist akzeptiert worden
        the suggestion has been accepted

c) *verbs which may take either* **sein** *or* **haben***:*

    i) Note that many verbs of motion can form their perfect tense with **sein** or **haben**, depending on the sense. Motion from one place to another requires **sein**, motion seen as a way of spending time takes **haben**:

        sie sind nach Griechenland gesegelt
        they sailed to Greece

        im Urlaub hat er jeden Tag gesegelt
        on holiday he went sailing every day

    There is a modern tendency not to make this distinction:

        wir sind über den See geschwommen
        we swam across the lake

    and:

        wir sind den ganzen Tag geschwommen
        we swam all day

    instead of:

        wir haben den ganzen Tag geschwommen
        we swam all day

    The latter is still perfectly correct, however.

Verbs which still normally keep this distinction in usage
between sein and haben are:

paddeln	**reiten**	**rudern**	**segeln**	**tanzen**
to paddle	to ride	to row	to sail	to dance

ii) Some verbs of motion can be used both transitively and
intransitively; in the first case they are conjugated with haben,
in the second with sein:

gestern hat er den Wagen gefahren
he drove the car yesterday

sie ist nach Hause gefahren
she drove home

er hat das Rohr gebogen	**sie ist um die Ecke gebogen**
he bent the pipe	she went round the corner

iii) Note similar distinctions:

er ist mir gefolgt	**er hat mir gefolgt**
he followed me	he obeyed me
der See ist gefroren	**ich habe gefroren**
the lake has frozen	I was freezing

iv) As a rule, liegen, sitzen and stehen are conjugated with haben
in north Germany and with sein in south Germany and Austria.

2 The order of infinitives and past participles

a) In tenses formed with an auxiliary verb – sein, haben, werden and
the modals – the auxiliary verb comes in second position in the
sentence but the past participle and/or infinitive comes at the
end of the clause:

wir sind gestern gefahren	**das kann ich nicht sagen**
we travelled yesterday	I can't say
es wird gerade gebaut	
it's just being built	

b) If there is both a past participle and an infinitive, the past participle comes first:

sie werden früher gefahren sein
they must have gone earlier

c) The infinitive of a modal verb used as a past participle and the past participle of werden come after the infinitive or past participle of the main verb:

das hättest du voraussehen können
you should have foreseen that

es ist noch nicht gebaut worden
it hasn't been built yet

d) In the future perfect passive the past participle is followed by worden and then sein:

es wird sicher bis Montag gefunden worden sein
I'm sure it will have been found by Monday

e) In the future perfect plus a modal verb the past participle is followed by the infinitive of sein or haben and then the infinitive of the modal:

er wird es gefunden haben müssen
he will have had to have found it

Note that these last two forms are often regarded as clumsy (*see* p 129).

f) Special word order in subordinate clauses

When two infinitive forms occur in a subordinate clause then the finite verb comes before them:

weißt du, dass ich dich habe kommen sehen?
do you know I saw you coming?

er sagte, dass er mich nicht hat verstehen können
he said he hadn't been able to understand me

3 Prefixes

a) *inseparable*

The inseparable prefixes are:

be   emp   ent   er   ge   miss   ver   zer

In pronunciation they are not stressed. They never separate from the verb. A verb with such a prefix has no ge- in the past participle.

b) *separable*

i) All other common prefixes are separable with the exception of the group mentioned in c) below. When they are attached to the verb they are stressed in pronunciation.

In statements, questions and imperatives these prefixes separate from the verb and are placed at the end of the clause. This does not apply in subordinate clauses where the finite verb is also at the end. In these cases the prefix and verb are joined:

kommst du mit?   **kommen Sie mit!**
are you coming?   come with me
sie fangen an
they're beginning
but: **weißt du, wann sie anfangen?**
do you know when they begin?

ii) The past participle for verbs with a separable prefix is formed with the ge coming between the prefix and verb stem:
anfangen – angefangen   **beibringen – beigebracht**

iii) When a verb with a separable prefix is in the infinitive form and is used with zu, the zu comes between the prefix and the verb stem:
er versuchte, den Weg abzukürzen
he tried to take a short cut

um die Zeit gut auszunutzen
so as to make good use of the time

c) *separable or inseparable*

durch   hinter   über   um   unter   wider   voll

can be either separable or inseparable prefixes. In most such cases
the separable and inseparable verbs have different meanings:

der Gärtner gräbt den Dung unter
the gardener digs the dung in

but:

er untergräbt seine Gesundheit
he is undermining his health

Usually the separable verb has a concrete, physical meaning, the
inseparable verb a figurative meaning.

wieder is always separable except in **wiederholen** in the sense of
'to repeat':

ich habe sie nie wiedergesehen   **sie wiederholten die Lektion**
I never saw her again   they repeated the lesson

d) *double prefixes*

i) In verbs which already have an inseparable prefix to which a
separable one is added (eg **ab-be-rufen**) the separable prefix still
separates, the **zu** is inserted between separable and inseparable
prefix *but* the past participle has no **ge-**:

die Regierung beruft den Botschafter ab
the government recalls its ambassador

die Regierung beabsichtigt, den Botschafter abzuberufen
the government intends to recall its ambassador

der Botschafter wurde abberufen
the ambassador was recalled

ii) Verbs formed by the combination of inseparable prefix +
separable prefix + verb (eg **be-ab-sichtigen**) are inseparable:

er beabsichtigt, morgen zu kommen
he intends to come tomorrow

C USE OF TENSES AND MOODS

1 The present tense

a) The present tense is used

    i) to express present states or actions:

       ich fühle mich schlecht   **der Arzt gibt mir eine Spritze**
       I feel ill   the doctor is giving me an injection

    ii) to express general or universal truths:

       Sabine hört gern Rockmusik   **Zeit ist Geld**
       Sabine likes listening to rock music   time is money

    iii) for firm intentions, refusals and for orders as an alternative to the imperative:

       ich mache das   **das Auto springt nicht an**
       I'll do it   the car won't start
       du gehst sofort ins Bett!
       you're to go to bed at once
       ich bleibe keine Minute länger hier!
       I won't stay here a minute longer

       This tense is often translated by either the English present or the present continuous:

       es regnet jeden Tag   **es regnet**
       it rains every day   it is raining

b) In German the present tense is the most common way of expressing the future:

    ich bin gleich zurück   **nächste Woche ist alles vorbei**
    I'll be right back   it'll all be over by next week
    du bekommst einen Brief
    you'll be getting a letter

c) With the conjunctions **seit** and **seitdem** and adverbial phrases using the preposition **seit** the present tense is used to express actions or states starting in the past and continuing into the present:

seit(dem) er die Tabletten nimmt, geht es ihm viel besser
since he has been taking the tablets he has been much better

er wartet seit zehn Uhr
he has been waiting since ten o'clock

d) The historic present is more common in German than in English. It is used to enliven a narrative of past events in written or spoken German:

ich liege auf der Couch - da kommt der Peter und gießt mir Wasser über den Kopf
there I was lying on the sofa when in came Peter and poured water over my head

It is also used for newspaper headlines and historical notes:
DIE QUEEN BESUCHT BERLIN
THE QUEEN VISITS BERLIN

1814: Napoleon entkommt aus der Haft
1814: Napoleon escapes

2 The imperfect tense

a) The imperfect tense is the standard tense for stories, novels and newspaper reports.

er ging die Straße entlang
he went along the road

der russische Außenminister traf gestern in Berlin ein
the Russian foreign minister arrived in Berlin yesterday

b) The imperfect tense is the one most commonly used (less so in southern Germany) with **sein, haben** and the modal verbs when referring to the past:

das war klasse!
that was great!

ich konnte es kaum glauben
I could hardly believe it

c) Note the following use of the imperfect with seit(dem):

seit(dem) er in Hamburg wohnte, hatte er …
since he had been living in Hamburg, he had …

3 The perfect tense

The perfect tense is the standard tense for conversation when talking about the past (except when using haben, sein and the modals as shown in 2.):

hast du ihn gesehen?
did you see him?

wann ist sie angekommen?
when did she arrive?

This does not mean to say that the imperfect cannot be used in German conversation. If, for example, you are relating a series of events then it is quite in order to use the imperfect (it's like telling a story). But for single utterances as in the above two examples, the use of the imperfect would sound odd.

4 The pluperfect tense

The pluperfect is used for events that happened before a particular time in the past:

nachdem wir den Film gesehen hatten, gingen wir ins Café
after we had seen the film we went to a café

5 The future and future perfect tenses

a) The future is used to express future matters but is less common in German than in English (*see* 1b *above*). The future as in:

ich werde ihn morgen treffen
I'm going to meet him tomorrow

is very often expressed by the present:

ich treffe ihn morgen
I'm meeting him tomorrow

b) It is also used to express suppositions about the present:

er hört mich nicht, er wird das Radio anhaben
he can't hear me, he's probably got the radio on

c) The future perfect is used to refer to an event that will be completed at some stage in the future:

ich werde das Buch bis Montag gelesen haben
I'll have read the book by Monday

It is also commonly used in German to express a supposition as in b) above:

er wird es vergessen haben
he'll have forgotten it

6 The passive

In the passive the active form ('he did it') is inverted so that the object becomes subject ('it was done by him').

a) There are two forms of the passive in German: the passive of action a nd the passive of state. The first (formed with **werden**) emphasises the action that was carried out, the second (formed with **sein**) denotes the result:

die Vase wurde zerbrochen   **die Vase ist zerbrochen**
the vase was broken   the vase is broken

When an agent is mentioned (who it was done by) the passive formed with **werden** must be used:

diese Wohnungen werden von der Stadt gebaut
these flats are being built by the council

but: **unser Haus ist schon gebaut**
        our house is already built

b) Verbs that take the dative or that are followed by a preposition cannot form the passive in this way and so a passive construction is usually avoided. For example:

sie sind ihm gefolgt
he was followed by them

When a passive is used with such verbs, note the difference from English:

mir wurde gesagt
I was told

c) Intransitive verbs can be transformed into an impersonal passive in which there is commonly no agent expressed:

es wurde getanzt
there was dancing

d) The agent (the subject of the verb in its active form) is usually referred to by the preposition von:

er wurde von seinem besten Freund betrogen
he was betrayed by his best friend

durch is most often used when the agent is not a person:

die Ernte wurde durch Hagel vernichtet
the harvest was destroyed by hail

ich wurde durch den Verkehr aufgehalten
I was held up by traffic

e) Note the use of man to replace a passive construction where a sentence such as 'it had been completely forgotten about' can be expressed either by:

es war völlig vergessen worden

or by:

man hatte es völlig vergessen

f) The passive can also be expressed by lassen:

das lässt sich machen   **er ließ sich nicht überreden**
that can be done   he couldn't be persuaded

g) The infinitive with zu can also be used to express the passive:

wie ist das zu erklären?   **er war nicht zu verstehen**
how is that to be explained?   he couldn't be understood

7 The imperative

a) The imperative is used to express requests and can range from a peremptory demand to a polite suggestion:

bleiben Sie stehen!
stop!

komm doch her!
come here!

sieh dir den kleinen Bengel an!
just look at the little rascal!

hören Sie nicht auf!
don't stop!

There is normally an exclamation mark, even after polite requests.

b) In the wir form, it is used for suggestions:

gehen wir!
let's go!

machen wir es uns gemütlich!
let's make ourselves comfortable

c) The infinitive is an alternative imperative, usually for fairly peremptory commands, for example in road signs *etc*:

links fahren!
drive on the left

nicht hinauslehnen!
do not lean out

8 The subjunctive

a) In spite of the fact that certain forms of the subjunctive are felt to be stilted (and are often replaced by the indicative or the würde form), it is still widely used in German:

   i) in conversation for conditional statements and with the modal verbs and:

   ii) in formal German, eg news bulletins, for reported statements.

The subjunctive gives the verb a mood of uncertainty, improbability or unreality. Thus it is mainly used for conditional statements, to express what might have been or what might, but probably will not, be; and for reported speech where it shows that what is reported was said by someone else and the speaker is not guaranteeing it to be a true statement.

b) The use of the subjunctive in conditional sentences

   i) Conditional sentences contain a main clause and an 'if' (wenn) clause. Conditional clauses in the present tense do not require the subjunctive; they state what will happen if some condition is fulfilled:

     wenn es morgen regnet, arbeite ich zu Hause
     if it rains tomorrow, I'll work at home

   ii) Conditions with the imperfect subjunctive in the main clause and in the wenn clause suggest the condition is unlikely to be fulfilled:

     wenn ich mehr Zeit hätte, ginge ich öfter spazieren
     if I had more time, I would go for more walks

   iii) The use of the würde forms

     The verb in the example above could be replaced by a würde form (the conditional):

     wenn ich mehr Zeit hätte, würde ich öfter spazieren gehen
     wäre and hätte are normally preferred to sein würde and haben würde.

     Note the possibility of omitting the wenn when there is inversion of subject and verb:

     hätte ich mehr Zeit, ginge ich öfter spazieren

   iv) Conditions with the pluperfect subjunctive in both clauses indicate what might have happened but did not:

     wenn er mich gefragt hätte, hätte ich ihm das Geld geliehen
     if he had asked me, I would have lent him the money

     The substitution of würde forms is also possible here, though less common.

   v) A wenn clause with the subjunctive can be used by itself in the sense of 'if only':

     wenn es nur schon Weihnachten wäre
     if only it were Christmas

c) The subjunctive with als ob and als wenn

The als ob or als wenn ('as if') construction expresses something which is regarded as uncertain or misleading and normally uses the subjunctive, although in spoken German the indicative can be used:

er tut, als ob er uns nicht gesehen hätte
he behaves as if he hadn't seen us

d) The subjunctive can be used in a main clause alone for instructions in mathematics and cookery:

man nehme fünf Eier
take five eggs

and with leben meaning 'long live' or 'three cheers for'
es lebe die Revolution!   **er lebe hoch!**
long live the revolution!   three cheers for him!

e) The subjunctive can also be used for questions and requests to make them less blunt and therefore more polite:

ich hätte eine Frage   **hätten Sie fünf Minuten für mich?**
might I ask a question?   could you spare me five minutes?

f) The subjunctive can be used for suggestions in the phrase wie wäre es mit ... ('how about ...?'):

wie wär's mit einem Glas Wein?
how about a glass of wine?

g) For the idiomatic uses of the subjunctive of modal verbs, see the section on modal verbs below.

h) The subjunctive in indirect speech

i) Indirect speech is the name given to statements or questions spoken by one person and reported by someone else:
he said, 'I will go there' → he said he would go there

The indirect speech is usually contained in a clause following a verb of speaking or asking. In German, such clauses are the only ones where the introductory **dass** may be omitted; if there is no **dass** normal word order is maintained:

er sagte, dass er kommen würde   **er sagte, er würde kommen**
he said he would come   he said he would come

ii) Indirect speech without the subjunctive
In German, direct speech is usually put into indirect speech by using the subjunctive, but if the verb of saying or asking is in the present tense, then the indicative is more common:

er sagt, dass er kommt
he says he's coming

In colloquial German the subjunctive is often avoided and the indicative retained in the tense used in direct speech:

er hat gesagt, dass er kommt
he said he would come

iii) Indirect speech with the subjunctive
The choice of tense for the indirect statement depends on the tense of the original direct speech as shown in the following table:

indicative tense of direct speech	subjunctive tense of indirect speech
present	present, imperfect
imperfect, perfect or pluperfect	perfect, pluperfect
future	future, **würde** + infinitive

Examples

ich finde es schwierig
I find it difficult

er hat gesagt, er finde/fände es schwierig
he said he found it difficult

ich fand es schwierig
ich habe es schwierig gefunden
ich hatte es schwierig gefunden

er hat gesagt, er habe/hätte es schwierig gefunden

ich werde es schwierig finden	er hat gesagt, er werde/würde es schwierig finden

iv) The choice of subjunctive tense in indirect speech

Written German

The preferred tenses in formal written German are the present subjunctive, the imperfect subjunctive and the future subjunctive (the first ones given in each of the examples above).

The main exceptions occur when the form of the subjunctive is identical to the indicative form it is replacing. In such cases the alternative form given above is used:

sie sagten, sie fänden (*not* finden) es schwierig
sie sagten, sie hätten (*not* haben) es schwierig gefunden
sie sagten, sie würden (*not* werden) es schwierig finden

If the present and imperfect subjunctives are both the same as the indicatives, the imperfect subjunctive is preferred:

sie sagten, sie arbeiteten (*not* arbeiten) fleißig

Spoken German

The preferred tenses in spoken German are the imperfect subjunctive, pluperfect subjunctive and würde + infinitive forms (the second choices given in the examples above). The würde + infinitive form is very commonly used instead of the imperfect subjunctive for verbs other than sein and haben:

sie sagte: "Ich wohne hier"	sie sagte, sie würde hier wohnen
she said, "I live here"	she said she lived here

9 The uses of the infinitive

The infinitive can be used together with certain verbs without any connecting link; in all other cases it is connected to the verb, noun or adjective phrase with zu.

a) *the infinitive without* zu

The infinitive is used without zu with modal verbs, and with certain verbs of perception, causation and instruction:

dürfen	to be allowed to
können	to be able to
mögen	to like to
müssen	to have to
sollen	to be supposed to
wollen	to want to
fühlen	to feel
hören	to hear
sehen	to see
spüren	to feel
heißen	to order to
lassen	to make, cause to; to allow to
machen	to make
helfen	to help to
lehren	to teach to
lernen	to learn to

   i) modals

   ich darf das nicht tun
   I'm not allowed to do that

   das muss heute getan werden
   it has to be done today

   er will es gesehen haben
   he claims to have seen it

   ii) The verbs of perception, causation and instruction normally have an object (in the dative with helfen) as well as the infinitive:

   er fühlte sein Herz schlagen
   he felt his heart beating

   ich sah ihn fallen
   I saw him fall

   er spürte eine Wut in sich aufsteigen
   he felt his anger rising

   hörst du ihn kommen?
   can you hear him coming?

   er machte die Leute aufhorchen
   he made the people sit up and listen

er hieß die Soldaten warten (*literary German*)
he told the soldiers to wait
sie ließ die Schüler früh nach Hause gehen
she allowed the children to go home early
Montag lasse ich den Wagen waschen
on Monday I'll get the car washed
sie haben mir aufräumen geholfen   **wer hat dich schwimmen gelehrt?**
they helped me tidy up   who taught you to swim?
er lernt gerade Auto fahren
he's just learning to drive

Note

When **helfen**, **lehren** and **lernen** are followed by an infinitive which has its own object or an adverb with it, the tendency is to use **zu**.

Compare:

der Blindenhund hilft ihm gehen
the guide dog helps him to walk

and:

der Blindenhund hilft ihm, die Straße zu überqueren
the guide dog helps him to cross the road

---

iii) The infinitive after **lassen** (and less commonly after **sehen**, **hören** and **heißen**) often has a passive sense:

er ließ das Zimmer streichen
he had the room painted

Compare this with the following use of **lassen**:

er ließ mich das Zimmer streichen
he got me to paint the room

lassen is used in this way as a reflexive (*see* p 167):

das lässt sich machen
that can be done

iv) After bleiben, verbs of sitting, standing, lying *etc* are in the infinitive without zu:

bleib sitzen!   **er blieb auf dem Boden liegen**
stay seated   he remained lying on the ground

v) brauchen is normally used with zu + infinitive in standard German but is also sometimes used without zu, especially in spoken German:

das brauchst du nicht an(zu)nehmen
you don't have to accept that

vi) kommen, gehen and schicken are used without zu with verbs denoting activities:

kommst du morgen schwimmen?
are you coming swimming tomorrow?

er hat die Kinder einkaufen geschickt
he sent the children out shopping

Note

• Past participle: when heißen, lassen, sehen and hören are used together with another infinitive, then it is normal to use the infinitive forms (heißen, lassen, sehen, hören) rather than the past participle forms (geheißen, gelassen, gesehen, gehört):

er hat mich kommen sehen
he saw me coming
er hat das Feuer ausgehen lassen
he let the fire go out

• Special word order: in subordinate clauses the finite verb precedes two infinitives at the end of a sentence:

weil er dich hat kommen lassen
because he got you to come

b) *the infinitive with* zu

   i) After nouns:

     hast du Lust mitzuspielen?
     would you like to join in the game?

   ii) After adjectives:

     ich war froh, ihn gesehen zu haben
     I was glad to have seen him

   iii) After past participles:

     er war erstaunt, mich zu sehen
     he was astonished to see me

   iv) After the prepositions um, (an)statt, and ohne:

     um ... zu is used to express purpose:

     er zahlte mehr, um einen besseren Platz zu bekommen
     he paid more to get a better seat

     um ... zu is also used after genug ('enough') and zu ('too') +
     adjective:

     du bist alt genug, um das zu wissen
     you're old enough to know that

     er ist zu schwach, um Nein zu sagen
     he's too weak to say no

     (an)statt zu ('instead of'):

     (an)statt zu feuern, ließ er die Waffe fallen
     he dropped his gun instead of shooting

     ohne zu ('without')

     er ging vorbei, ohne zu grüßen
     he went past without saying hello

    Note that after nouns, adjectives, past participles and
    prepositions the subject of the main verb must also be the
    subject of the infinitive.

v) After verbs:

es begann sofort zu regnen   **wir versuchten ihn aufzuhalten**
it immediately started to rain   we tried to stop him

Verbs which are followed by a preposition often, but not always, have **da(r)** + preposition before the **zu** + infinitive phrase:

ich freue mich darauf, euch zu sehen
I'm looking forward to seeing you

er ärgerte sich (darüber), den Zug verpasst zu haben
he was annoyed at missing the train

After **sein** the infinitive with **zu** has a passive meaning:

er ist nicht zu ersetzen   **der Schmerz war nicht zu ertragen**
he is irreplaceable   the pain was unbearable

vi) *For the punctuation of the infinitival clause see* **pp 250–251**

c) *For the use of the infinitive as imperative see section* **7c** *above.*

d) The infinitive can also be used as a noun. Such nouns begin with a capital letter and are always neuter; they generally denote the action of the verb:

das Schwimmen
swimming

They can be compounded with a noun object:

das Autofahren
car driving

They are often used with **bei**:

er wurde beim Mogeln ertappt
he was caught cheating

10 The uses of the participles

a) *present participle*

i) The present participle is used mainly as an adjective either before the noun or after **sein**:

eine ansteckende Krankheit   **diese Krankheit ist ansteckend**
an infectious disease   this disease is infectious

ii) It can occasionally be used as an adverb after other verbs:

sie redete überzeugend
she talked convincingly

iii) The present participle preceded by zu – which can have further words or phrases before it – can be used as an extended adjective before the noun:

kein einfach zu lösendes Problem
a problem that is/was not easy to solve

eine schwer zu begreifende Entscheidung
a decision that is/was difficult to comprehend

iv) Phrases using present participles in the following way mainly occur in literary usage:

die Zeitung zerknüllend, stand er auf
crumpling the paper, he stood up

b) *past participle*

i) Apart from its use to form tenses, the past participle is also used as an adjective:

der verdammte Bengel
that damned rascal

ii) Its use to form extended adjective phrases before the noun is widespread in formal written German:

der erst neulich gestürzte Präsident
the recently deposed president

iii) Phrases using past participles in the following way mainly occur in literary usage:

vom Einbruch der Nacht überrascht, musste er im Freien schlafen
being suddenly overtaken by nightfall, he had to sleep out of doors

but:

a small number of verbs are in common use in such participial constructions, for example: **vorausgesetzt, gesagt, ausgenommen:**

genau gesagt
to be precise

dein Bruder ausgenommen, fahren alle mit dem Zug
except for your brother everyone is going by train

iv) The past participle is used idiomatically with kommen:

er kam gelaufen
he came running

11 The usages of modal verbs (*conjugation see* pp 127-31)

a) dürfen

i) dürfen expresses permission ('to be allowed to'):

niemand darf das Haus verlassen
no-one may leave the house

darf ich Sie stören?   **das darfst du nicht sagen**
may I interrupt?   you shouldn't/mustn't say that

ii) dürfen in the imperfect subjunctive expresses a probable supposition:

er dürfte gestern krank gewesen sein
he was probably ill yesterday

das dürfte wohl stimmen
that might well be true

iii) dürfen in the negative translates English 'must not':

du darfst nicht bei Rot über die Straße gehen
you must not cross the road when the lights are red

iv) Idiomatic uses:

was darf es sein?
(in shop) what can I do for you?
(getting a drink) what can I get you?

b) können

i) können expresses ability:

er kann gut schwimmen   **kannst du Spanisch?**
he can swim well   can you speak Spanish?

kannst du Gitarre spielen?
do you know how to play the guitar?

leider können wir nicht kommen
I'm afraid we can't come

ii) **können** expresses possibility:

er kann den Einbrecher gesehen haben
he might have seen the burglar

du kannst recht haben
you might be right

iii) **können** is often used in place of dürfen to express permission, especially in spoken German:

du kannst machen, was du willst
you can do as you like

iv) **können** is used in the idiom etwas/jemand (gut) leiden können:

ich kann diese Musik gut leiden
I like this music

c) **mögen**

Note that mögen is also used with an object, meaning 'to like':

ich mag keine Rockmusik
I don't like rock music

i) The commonest use of mögen is to express wish or desire. In this usage it is most often seen in the imperfect subjunctive:

ich möchte ihn kennenlernen   **ich möchte ein Eis**
I'd like to get to know him   I'd like an ice cream

but it is also used in the present:

ich mag nicht länger bleiben
I don't want to stay any longer

ii) **mögen** is used to express supposition or possibility:

du magst recht haben   **wer mag das sein?**
you may well be right   who can/might that be?

er mochte etwa zwanzig sein
he was probably about twenty

iii) **mögen** expresses concession:

das mag sein, aber es gefällt mir nicht
that may be so, but I don't like it

iv) The imperfect subjunctive of **mögen** is also used as a polite alternative to the imperative:

Besucher möchten das Schloss bitte vor sechs Uhr verlassen
visitors are asked to leave the castle before six o'clock

v) It is used in the idiom **jemand (gut) leiden mögen**:

ich mag ihn gut leiden
I like him

d) **müssen**

i) **müssen** is used to express necessity:

ich muss schon sagen ...   **ich musste mich beeilen**
I really must say ...   I had to hurry

ii) It can also express supposition:

jemand muss es versteckt haben
someone must have hidden it

iii) In the imperfect subjunctive it expresses a wish or hope:

das müsste eigentlich passen   **Geld müsste man haben!**
that ought to fit   it would be nice to have money

iv) The negative of **müssen** is not the same as 'must not' in English:

du musst nicht kommen
you don't have to come

In order to say 'you must not come', German uses **dürfen**:

du darfst nicht kommen
you must not come

e) **sollen**

i) **sollen** expresses duty or obligation:

du sollst nicht töten   **er sollte seinem Vater helfen**
thou shalt not kill   he ought to help his father
ich hätte es früher tun sollen
I ought to have done it earlier

> ### Note
>
> There is sometimes a distinction in this sense between the present and the imperfect subjunctive. The present tense implies that the obligation is imposed from the outside while the imperfect subjunctive implies that it comes from within the speaker:
>
> **ich soll nicht rauchen**
> I shouldn't smoke
> (= *my doctor's told me*)
>
> **ich sollte nicht rauchen**
> I shouldn't smoke
> (= *I know it's bad for me*)

ii) sollen is used to express a rumour or generally held opinion:

dieser soll der beste sein
this one is supposed to be the best

es sollte heute regnen, hat aber nicht
it was supposed to rain today but didn't

iii) The imperfect tense of sollen can be used to express a future in the past:

das sollte ihn teuer zu stehen kommen
he was to pay dearly for it

das sollten wir später erfahren
we were to find that out later

f) wollen

i) wollen expresses intention or desire:

er will nur dein Bestes
he only wants the best for you

ich will sie heiraten
I'm determined to marry her

Note the use of wollen with non-personal subjects in the sense of 'to refuse to':

der Regen wollte nicht enden
the rain just wouldn't stop

der Motor wollte nicht anspringen
the engine refused to start

Note the construction with dass:

alle wollen, dass du kommst
everyone wants you to come

er will, dass ich ihm helfe
he wants me to help him

ii) wollen is used to express a claim made by someone and reported by the speaker:

er will das Geld gar nicht gesehen haben
he claims he never saw the money

er will alles besser wissen
he always thinks he knows best

iii) In the imperfect tense and followed by gerade it is the equivalent of 'to be about to':

er wollte gerade verschwinden
he was about to disappear

iv) wollen is used with the passive infinitive in the sense of 'must':

der Fall will vorsichtig behandelt werden
the case must be handled carefully

g) *The omission of the infinitive with the modal verb*

Infinitives expressing movement may be omitted when it is clear what is intended; this is usually when there is an adverb or adverbial phrase expressing direction:

du sollst sofort in die Schule   **ich muss heute nach Dortmund**
you are to go to school at once   I have to go to Dortmund today
ich darf nicht nach draußen
I'm not allowed out

h) *The alternative perfect and pluperfect forms of the modal verbs often have different meanings.*

er hat es tun sollen   **er soll es getan haben**
he was supposed to do it   he is supposed to have done it
er hat es tun müssen   **er muss es getan haben**
he had to do it   he must have done it

With können the distinction is less obvious from the English:

er hat es tun können   **er kann es getan haben**
he could have done it   he may have done it
(= had the opportunity)   *(= is a possible culprit)*

er hätte es tun können   er könnte es getan haben
he could have done it   he might have done it
(= if he had been willing)   *(= is a possible culprit)*

12 Impersonal verbs

a) Impersonal verbs are verbs which have **es** as the subject when **es** does not refer to any specific person, thing or action.

Compare:

es ist besser zu gehen
it's better to go (impersonal)

and:

dieses Buch? –es ist mein Lieblingsbuch
this book? –it's my favourite ('personal', **es** refers to the book)

Impersonal verbs can be divided into two groups, depending on whether the **es** is kept when the subject and verb are inverted:

es gibt kein Essen heute   **es ist mir schlecht**
heute gibt's kein Essen   **mir ist schlecht**
there's no food today   I feel ill

b) Apart from those listed under c) below, impersonal verbs and expressions retain the **es** in inversion. In some cases the **es** in inversion is optional. Below are some of the main types of impersonal verbs that keep the **es**:

Verbs of weather and similar phenomena:

es regnet	**es schneit**	**es hagelt**
it's raining	it's snowing	it's hailing
es donnert	**es blitzt**	**es friert**
it's thundering	there is lightning	it's freezing
es dunkelt	**es tagt**	**es dämmert**
it's getting dark	it's getting light	dawn/twilight is coming
es wird Sommer	**es spukt**	
summer is coming	there are ghosts about	
es brennt	**es zieht**	
there's a fire	there's a draught	

Note that some of these may be used to refer to persons:

es friert mich	**es ist mir kalt**
I'm freezing	I'm cold

This form is felt to be slightly stilted and inversion is common:

mich friert (es)	**mir ist (es) kalt**

The **es** may be kept but is usually omitted.

Verbs of noise:

es klingelt	there's a ring
es läutet	there's a ring
es klopft	there's a knock
es raschelt	there's a rustling

Other impersonal verbs:

es gefällt mir	I like it
es geht	it's all right
es gibt	there is/are
es handelt sich um	it is a matter of
es kommt darauf an	it depends

Note that **es war einmal** ('once upon a time') is never inverted.

c) Impersonal verbs where **es** is omitted in inversion

In expressions formed with **es ist** + adjectives expressing a state of mind, body or health the **es** is normally omitted in inversion:

ihm war traurig zumute	he felt sad
mir ist warm	I feel warm
mir wird besser	I'm getting better
ihr ist schlecht	she feels sick

In the impersonal passive the **es** is always omitted in inversion:

die ganze Nacht hindurch wurde getanzt
the dancing went on all night

Verbs indicating position omit the **es** in inversion; the most common are **liegen**, **sein** and **stehen**:

es steht in der Zeitung, dass …
in der Zeitung steht, dass …
it says in the paper that …

d) es gibt *or* es ist?

es gibt is the usual German translation for 'there is/are'; the verb is always in the singular:

gibt es einen Aufzug?	**zum Abendessen gibt es Forellen**
is there a lift?	there is trout for dinner

es gibt nie Ruhe hier
there's never any peace and quiet here

es ist/sind is only used when there is an indication of place or position.
Compare:

es ist Post da
the post has arrived

and:

heute gibt es keine Post
there's no post today

es ist/sind is particularly common when the presence is only temporary:

es sind zwei Mädchen an der Tür
there are two girls at the door

Note that es ist/sind loses the es in inversion:

in München war eine Demonstration
there was a demonstration in Munich

es ist/sind can be used for weather, but es gibt is also possible:

es war diesen Sommer wenig Sonne
es hat diesen Sommer wenig Sonne gegeben
there wasn't much sun this summer

13 Reflexive verbs

a) Reflexive verbs are verbs used with a reflexive pronoun which relates the action back to the subject:

I washed myself: 'myself' is the reflexive pronoun.

b) German has both accusative and dative reflexive pronouns:

PERSON	ACCUSATIVE	DATIVE
ich	mich	mir
du	dich	dir
er/sie/es	sich	sich
wir	uns	uns
ihr	euch	euch
Sie/sie	sich	sich

There are some German verbs which only occur as reflexives but for which the English equivalent contains no reflexive pronoun:

beeil dich!　　　　　　　　　　**ich habe mich dazu entschlossen**
hurry up!　　　　　　　　　　　　I have decided to do it

c) The position of the reflexive pronoun

The reflexive pronoun usually comes immediately after the verb:

mein Vater erinnert sich daran
my father remembers it

With inversion or when the finite verb is at the end it usually follows a pronoun subject but comes before a noun subject or other pronouns:

erinnert sich dein Vater daran?
does your father remember it?

erinnert er sich daran?　　　　**erinnert sich einer daran?**
does he remember it?　　　　　　does anyone remember it?

In an infinitive phrase the reflexive pronoun comes first:

ich muss nicht vergessen, mir ein neues Hemd zu kaufen
I mustn't forget to buy a new shirt

The reflexive cannot precede the finite verb in normal word order.

Note that all reflexive verbs form their perfect tense with **haben**. The conjugation is as for other verbs.

d) Usage

Reflexive pronouns are basically used to relate the action of the verb back to the subject:

ich wasche mich   **du schadest dir dabei bloß selbst**
I wash myself   you'll only harm yourself

In the plural the reflexive pronoun can be reciprocal and is often translated into English by 'each other':

wir sehen uns morgen
we'll see each other tomorrow

This can also be expressed by **einander**:

sie sehen einander jeden Tag
they see each other every day

The accusative reflexive pronoun is used with many verbs with the prefix ver- to express that the action of the verb has been done wrongly:

ich habe mich versprochen   **er hat sich verzählt**
I made a slip of the tongue   he miscounted

e) There is an impersonal reflexive construction which expresses in general whether an activity is pleasant or easy or not:

in Turnschuhen läuft es sich bequem
trainers are comfortable to run in

in einem weichen Bett schläft es sich schlecht
soft beds are bad for sleeping in

With the reflexive form of lassen the verb following has a passive sense:

das lässt sich leicht machen
that's easily done

The dative reflexive can be used to indicate that the object belongs to the subject of the verb:

ich wasche mir die Hände   **sie zog sich die Schuhe an**
I wash my hands   she put her shoes on

The dative reflexive is also used with many verbs to emphasise the subject's interest or involvement in the activity of the verb. In these cases the dative reflexive is usual but not obligatory:

den Film sehe ich mir bestimmt an
I'm certainly going to see that film

du solltest dir einen neuen Wagen kaufen
you should buy a new car

When a pronoun used with a preposition refers back to the subject the reflexive pronoun must be used. (It is only in the er/sie/es and Sie/sie forms that it is actually different from the regular pronoun):

vor sich sah er jemand laufen
he saw someone running in front of him(self)

er sah jemand hinter ihm
he saw someone behind him *(- 'him' not the same person as 'he')*

14 Verbs taking the dative

a) The dative is used for the indirect object and comes after many verbs of giving, sending, telling. Often the fact that the object is in the dative will be clear from the English equivalent:

bring mir die Teller!
bring the plates to me

But:

English often omits the 'to' as in: 'bring me the plates'.
German usage is sometimes different from English:

sagen Sie es mir!   **Sie wollten mich sprechen?**
tell me   you wanted to speak to me?

b) Many verbs take both a dative and an accusative object:

er hat mir alles erzählt
he told me everything

c) Verbs formed with the prefixes bei- and nach- and inseparable
   verbs with the prefix ent- with the basic meaning of 'to escape
   from' take the dative:

beistehen	to support
nachgeben	to give in to
entkommen	to escape from

d) Here is a list of many of the more common verbs that take
   a dative object. Verbs that fit into the categories above have
   largely been omitted:

auffallen	to strike, be noticed
ausweichen	to get out of the way of
befehlen	to order
begegnen	to meet
danken	to thank
dienen	to serve
drohen	to threaten
empfehlen	to recommend
erlauben	to allow
fehlen	to be lacking
folgen	to follow
gefallen	to please
gehorchen	to obey
gehören	to belong to

gelingen	to succeed
genügen	to be enough for
glauben	to believe
gratulieren	to congratulate
helfen	to help
misstrauen	to distrust
passen	to suit
raten	to advise
reichen	to be enough for
schaden	to harm
schmeicheln	to flatter
trauen	to trust
verbieten	to forbid
versichern	to assure
vertrauen	to trust
verzeihen	to forgive
vorstehen	to preside over
wehtun	to hurt
widersprechen	to contradict
widerstehen	to resist
zusehen	to watch
zustimmen	to agree to

15 Verbs with two accusative objects

A few verbs can be followed by two objects in the accusative. This is almost entirely restricted to kosten ('to cost'), lehren ('to teach'), nennen ('to call') and fragen ('to ask'):

> **das kann ihn den Kragen kosten**
> that might be his downfall

> **er nannte mich einen Dummkopf**
> he called me a fool

> **sie haben mich Schwieriges gefragt**
> they asked me difficult things

16 Verbs followed by prepositions

a) Many German verbs are followed by prepositions. Very often these are not the obvious ones from the English equivalent and should be learnt – along with the case if necessary – with the verb:

ich fürchte mich vor ihm
I'm afraid of him

Some verbs can be followed by different prepositions, usually with a change of meaning:

ich freue mich auf die Ferien
I'm looking forward to the holidays

sie hat sich über das Geschenk gefreut
she was pleased with the present

Such verbs often have a noun following the preposition. However, they can also be followed by an infinitive phrase or a subordinate clause – usually a **dass** clause. When they are followed by such an infinitive or clause it is very common to insert the preposition in the main clause with the prefix **da(r)-** before it:

ich erinnere mich an ihn
I remember him

ich erinnere mich daran, ihn gesehen zu haben
I remember seeing him

b) Here is a list of some of the more common verbs with prepositions:

i) an + *acc*

denken an	to think of *(have in one's mind)*
sich erinnern an	to remember
erinnern an	to remind
sich gewöhnen an	to become accustomed to

ii) **an** + *dat*

es fehlt an	there is a lack of
leiden an	to suffer from *(disease)*

iii) **auf** + *acc*

achtgeben auf	to pay attention to
aufpassen auf	to keep an eye on
sich beschränken auf	to restrict oneself to
sich freuen auf	to look forward to
hoffen auf	to hope for
reagieren auf	to react to
rechnen auf	to count on
sich verlassen auf	to rely upon
verzichten auf	to renounce
warten auf	to wait for

iv) **auf** + *dat*

bestehen auf	to insist upon

v) **aus** + *dat*

bestehen aus	to consist of

vi) **für** + *acc*

sich bedanken für	to say thank you for
sich einsetzen für	to do a lot for
sich entscheiden für	to decide in favour of
halten für	to consider
sich interessieren für	to be interested in
sorgen für	to look after

vii) **mit** + *dat*

aufhören mit	to stop doing
einverstanden sein mit	to be in agreement with
rechnen mit	to count on

viii) **nach** + *dat*

fragen nach	to ask for
schmecken nach	to taste of
suchen nach	to look for

ix) über + *acc*

sich freuen über	to be pleased at
lachen über	to laugh at
nachdenken über	to reflect upon

x) um + *acc*

sich kümmern um	to care for
sich sorgen um	to be worried about
es geht um	it is a matter of
es handelt sich um	it is a matter of

xi) unter + *dat*

leiden unter	to suffer from *(noise etc)*
verstehen unter	to understand by

xii) von + *dat*

abhängen von	to be dependent on
sich erholen von	to recuperate from
handeln von	to be about

xiii) vor + *dat*

sich fürchten vor	to be afraid of

xiv) zu + *dat*

beitragen zu	to contribute to
sich entschließen zu	to decide upon

17 List of strong verbs

Verbs with an asterisk (*) are conjugated with sein.

Verbs with a prefix take the same forms as the simple verbs (without the prefix), eg versprechen and aussprechen take the same forms as sprechen.

Past participles used after infinitives: er hätte nicht bleiben wollen (he wouldn't have wanted to stay). Compare this with: er hat nicht gewollt (he didn't want to).

Infinitive	English	Present Indicative *3rd pers sing*	Imperfect Indicative	Past Participle
backen	to bake	bäckt, backt	backte	gebacken
befehlen	to order	befiehlt	befahl	befohlen
beginnen	to begin	beginnt	begann	begonnen
beißen	to bite	beißt	biss	gebissen
bergen	to salvage, rescue	birgt	barg	geborgen
bersten	to burst	birst	barst	geborsten*
bewegen	to persuade	bewegt	bewog	bewogen
biegen	to bend, turn	biegt	bog	gebogen
bieten	to offer	bietet	bot	geboten
binden	to tie	bindet	band	gebunden
bitten	to ask	bittet	bat	gebeten
blasen	to blow	bläst	blies	geblasen
bleiben	to stay	bleibt	blieb	geblieben*
braten	to fry	brät	briet	gebraten
brechen	to break	bricht	brach	gebrochen
brennen	to burn	brennt	brannte	gebrannt
bringen	to bring	bringt	brachte	gebracht
denken	to think	denkt	dachte	gedacht
dreschen	to thresh	drischt	drosch	gedroschen
dringen	to penetrate, urge	dringt	drang	gedrungen*
dürfen	to be allowed to	darf	durfte	gedurft; *(after infinitive)* dürfen
empfangen	to receive	empfängt	empfing	empfangen
empfehlen	to recommend	empfiehlt	empfahl	empfohlen
empfinden	to feel	empfindet	empfand	empfunden
erschrecken	to be startled	erschreckt	erschrak	erschrocken*
essen	to eat	isst	aß	gegessen
fahren	to drive	fährt	fuhr	gefahren*

fallen	to fall	fällt	fiel	gefallen*
fangen	to catch	fängt	fing	gefangen
fechten	to fence	ficht	focht	gefochten
finden	to find	findet	fand	gefunden
flechten	to weave, twine	flicht	flocht	geflochten
fliegen	to fly	fliegt	flog	geflogen*
fliehen	to flee	flieht	floh	geflohen*
fließen	to flow	fließt	floss	geflossen*
fressen	to eat	frisst	fraß	gefressen
frieren	to freeze	friert	fror	gefroren
gebären	to give birth (to)	gebiert	gebar	geboren
geben	to give	gibt	gab	gegeben
gedeihen	to thrive	gedeiht	gedieh	gediehen*
gehen	to go	geht	ging	gegangen*
gelingen	to succeed	gelingt	gelang	gelungen*
gelten	to be valid	gilt	galt	gegolten
genesen	to recover, convalesce	genest	genas	genesen*
genießen	to enjoy	genießt	genoss	genossen
geschehen	to happen	geschieht	geschah	geschehen*
gewinnen	to win	gewinnt	gewann	gewonnen
gießen	to pour	gießt	goss	gegossen
gleichen	to resemble, be like	gleicht	glich	geglichen
gleiten	to glide	gleitet	glitt	geglitten*
glimmen	to glow	glimmt	glomm	geglommen
graben	to dig	gräbt	grub	gegraben
greifen	to grasp	greift	griff	gegriffen
haben	to have	hat	hatte	gehabt
halten	to hold	hält	hielt	gehalten
hängen	to hang	hängt	hing	gehangen
hauen	to hit, hew	haut	haute	gehauen
heben	to lift	hebt	hob	gehoben
heißen	to be called	heißt	hieß	geheißen
helfen	to help	hilft	half	geholfen

kennen	to know	kennt	kannte	gekannt
klingen	to sound	klingt	klang	geklungen
kneifen	to pinch	kneift	kniff	gekniffen
kommen	to come	kommt	kam	gekommen*
können	to be able to	kann	konnte	gekonnt; *(after infinitive)* können
kriechen	to crawl	kriecht	kroch	gekrochen*
laden	to load	lädt	lud	geladen
lassen	to leave, let	lässt	ließ	gelassen; *(after infinitive)* lassen
laufen	to run	läuft	lief	gelaufen*
leiden	to suffer	leidet	litt	gelitten
leihen	to lend, borrow	leiht	lieh	geliehen
lesen	to read	liest	las	gelesen
liegen	to lie	liegt	lag	gelegen
lügen	to tell lies	lügt	log	gelogen
mahlen	to grind	mahlt	mahlte	gemahlen
meiden	to avoid	meidet	mied	gemieden
melken	to milk	melkt	melkte	gemolken
messen	to measure	misst	maß	gemessen
misslingen	to fail	misslingt	misslang	misslungen*
mögen	to like	mag	mochte	gemocht; *(after infinitive)* mögen
müssen	to have to	muss	musste	gemusst; *(after infinitive)* müssen
nehmen	to take	nimmt	nahm	genommen
nennen	to call, name	nennt	nannte	genannt
pfeifen	to whistle	pfeift	pfiff	gepfiffen
preisen	to praise	preist	pries	gepriesen
quellen	to pour	quillt	quoll	gequollen*
raten	to guess, advise	rät	riet	geraten
reiben	to rub	reibt	rieb	gerieben

reißen	to rip	reißt	riss	gerissen
reiten	to ride	reitet	ritt	geritten
rennen	to run	rennt	rannte	gerannt*
riechen	to smell	riecht	roch	gerochen
ringen	to wrestle, struggle	ringt	rang	gerungen
rinnen	to run (liquid)	rinnt	rann	geronnen*
rufen	to call	ruft	rief	gerufen
salzen	to salt	salzt	salzte	gesalzen
saufen	to drink	säuft	soff	gesoffen
saugen	to suck	saugt	sog, saugte	gesogen, gesaugt
schaffen	to create	schafft	schuf	geschaffen
scheiden	to separate	scheidet	schied	geschieden
scheinen	to shine, seem	scheint	schien	geschienen
scheißen	to shit	scheißt	schiss	geschissen
schelten	to scold	schilt	schalt	gescholten
scheren	to shear	schert	schor	geschoren
schieben	to push	schiebt	schob	geschoben
schießen	to shoot	schießt	schoss	geschossen
schinden	to maltreat	schindet	schindete	geschunden
schlafen	to sleep	schläft	schlief	geschlafen
schlagen	to beat, hit	schlägt	schlug	geschlagen
schleichen	to creep	schleicht	schlich	geschlichen*
schleifen	to sharpen	schleift	schliff	geschliffen
schließen	to shut	schließt	schloss	geschlossen
schlingen	to tie	schlingt	schlang	geschlungen
schmeißen	to chuck	schmeißt	schmiss	geschmissen
schmelzen	to melt	schmilzt	schmolz	geschmolzen
schneiden	to cut	schneidet	schnitt	geschnitten
schreiben	to write	schreibt	schrieb	geschrieben
schreien	to shout	schreit	schrie	geschrien
schreiten	to stride	schreitet	schritt	geschritten*
schweigen	to be silent	schweigt	schwieg	geschwiegen
schwellen	to swell	schwillt	schwoll	geschwollen*
schwimmen	to swim	schwimmt	schwamm	geschwommen*

schwinden	to fade, dwindle	schwindet	schwand	geschwunden*
schwingen	to swing	schwingt	schwang	geschwungen
schwören	to swear	schwört	schwor	geschworen
sehen	to see	sieht	sah	gesehen; *(after infinitive)* **sehen**
sein	to be	**ist**	war	gewesen*
senden	to send	sendet	sandte	gesandt
singen	to sing	singt	sang	gesungen
sinken	to sink	sinkt	sank	gesunken*
sinnen	to ponder	sinnt	sann	gesonnen
sitzen	to sit	sitzt	saß	gesessen
sollen	to be supposed to	**soll**	sollte	gesollt; *(after infinitive)* **sollen**
spalten	to split	spaltet	spaltete	gespalten, gespaltet
speien	to spit, spew	speit	spie	gespien
spinnen	to spin	spinnt	spann	gesponnen
sprechen	to speak	spricht	sprach	gesprochen
sprießen	to sprout	sprießt	spross, sprießte	gesprossen*
springen	to jump	springt	sprang	gesprungen*
stechen	to sting	sticht	stach	gestochen
stecken	to be stuck	steckt	steckte, stak	gesteckt
stehen	to stand	steht	stand	gestanden
stehlen	to steal	stiehlt	stahl	gestohlen
steigen	to climb	steigt	stieg	gestiegen*
sterben	to die	stirbt	starb	gestorben*
stoßen	to push	stößt	stieß	gestoßen
streichen	to paint, spread, stroke, delete	streicht	strich	gestrichen
streiten	to argue	streitet	stritt	gestritten
tragen	to carry, wear	trägt	trug	getragen
treffen	to meet, hit	trifft	traf	getroffen

treiben	to drive, float	treibt	trieb	getrieben
treten	to kick, tread	tritt	trat	getreten
trinken	to drink	trinkt	trank	getrunken
trügen	to deceive	trügt	trog	getrogen
tun	to do	tut	tat	getan
verderben	to spoil	verdirbt	verdarb	verdorben
verdrießen	to annoy	verdrießt	verdross	verdrossen
vergessen	to forget	vergisst	vergaß	vergessen
verlieren	to lose	verliert	verlor	verloren
verschleißen	to wear out	verschleißt	verschliss	verschlissen
verzeihen	to forgive	verzeiht	verzieh	verziehen
wachsen	to grow	wächst	wuchs	gewachsen*
waschen	to wash	wäscht	wusch	gewaschen
weben	to weave	webt	webte, wob	gewebt, gewoben
weichen	to yield	weicht	wich	gewichen*
weisen	to show	weist	wies	gewiesen
wenden	to turn	wendet	wendete, wandte	gewendet, gewandt
werben	to advertise, recruit	wirbt	warb	geworben
werden	to become	wird	wurde	geworden*; *(after past participle)* worden
werfen	to throw	wirft	warf	geworfen
wiegen	to weigh	wiegt	wog	gewogen
winden	to wind	windet	wand	gewunden
winken	to wave	winkt	winkte	gewinkt, gewunken
wissen	to know	weiß	wusste	gewusst
wollen	to want to	will	wollte	gewollt; *(after infinitive)* wollen
wringen	to wring	wringt	wrang	gewrungen
ziehen	to pull	zieht	zog	gezogen
zwingen	to force	zwingt	zwang	gezwungen

D CONJUGATION TABLES

The following verbs provide the main patterns of conjugation including the conjugation of some common irregular verbs. They are arranged in alphabetical order.

Verbs with auxiliary **haben** (*see* pp 134–35)	BRAUCHEN
Verbs with auxiliary **sein** (*see* pp 135–36)	STÜRZEN
Reflexive verbs (*see* pp 165–67)	SICH BEEILEN
Separable verbs (*see* pp 139–40)	ABLEHNEN
Auxiliaries (*see* p 8)	HABEN
	SEIN
	WERDEN
Verbs with special endings (*see* p 114)	
Verbs ending in -den/-ten/-men/-nen	WARTEN
Verbs ending in -ln/-rn	ÄRGERN
Verbs ending in -ssen	PASSEN
Modal verbs (*see* pp 127–31, 157–62)	DÜRFEN
	KÖNNEN
	MÖGEN
	MÜSSEN
	SOLLEN
	WOLLEN

'Chambers German Verbs', a fully comprehensive list of German verbs and their conjugations, is also available in this series.

ABLEHNEN *to reject, decline*

PRESENT
ich lehne ab
du lehnst ab
er/sie lehnt ab
wir lehnen ab
ihr lehnt ab
Sie lehnen ab
sie lehnen ab

IMPERFECT
ich lehnte ab
du lehntest ab
er/sie lehnte ab
wir lehnten ab
ihr lehntet ab
Sie lehnten ab
sie lehnten ab

FUTURE
ich werde ablehnen
du wirst ablehnen
er/sie wird ablehnen
wir werden ablehnen
ihr werdet ablehnen
Sie werden ablehnen
sie werden ablehnen

PERFECT
ich habe abgelehnt
du hast abgelehnt
er/sie hat abgelehnt
wir haben abgelehnt
ihr habt abgelehnt
Sie haben abgelehnt
sie haben abgelehnt

PLUPERFECT
ich hatte abgelehnt
du hattest abgelehnt
er/sie hatte abgelehnt
wir hatten abgelehnt
ihr hattet abgelehnt
Sie hatten abgelehnt
sie hatten abgelehnt

CONDITIONAL
ich würde ablehnen
du würdest ablehnen
er/sie würde ablehnen
wir würden ablehnen
ihr würdet ablehnen
Sie würden ablehnen
sie würden ablehnen

SUBJUNCTIVE

PRESENT
ich lehne ab
du lehnest ab
er/sie lehne ab
wir lehnen ab
ihr lehnet ab
Sie lehnen ab
sie lehnen ab

PERFECT
ich habe abgelehnt
du habest abgelehnt
er/sie habe abgelehnt
wir haben abgelehnt
ihr habet abgelehnt
Sie haben abgelehnt
sie haben abgelehnt

INFINITIVE

PRESENT
ablehnen

PAST
abgelehnt haben

PARTICIPLE

PRESENT
ablehnend

PAST
abgelehnt

IMPERFECT
ich lehnte ab
du lehntest ab
er/sie lehnte ab
wir lehnten ab
ihr lehntet ab
Sie lehnten ab
sie lehnten ab

PLUPERFECT
ich hätte abgelehnt
du hättest abgelehnt
er/sie hätte abgelehnt
wir hätten abgelehnt
ihr hättet abgelehnt
Sie hätten abgelehnt
sie hätten abgelehnt

IMPERATIVE

lehn(e) ab!
lehnt ab!
lehnen Sie ab!
lehnen wir ab!

FUTURE PERFECT
ich werde abgelehnt haben
du wirst abgelehnt haben *etc*

ÄRGERN *to annoy*

PRESENT	IMPERFECT	FUTURE
ich ärgere	ich ärgerte	ich werde ärgern
du ärgerst	du ärgertest	du wirst ärgern
er/sie ärgert	er/sie ärgerte	er/sie wird ärgern
wir ärgern	wir ärgerten	wir werden ärgern
ihr ärgert	ihr ärgertet	ihr werdet ärgern
Sie ärgern	Sie ärgerten	Sie werden ärgern
sie ärgern	sie ärgerten	sie werden ärgern

PERFECT	PLUPERFECT	CONDITIONAL
ich habe geärgert	ich hatte geärgert	ich würde ärgern
du hast geärgert	du hattest geärgert	du würdest ärgern
er/sie hat geärgert	er/sie hatte geärgert	er/sie würde ärgern
wir haben geärgert	wir hatten geärgert	wir würden ärgern
ihr habt geärgert	ihr hattet geärgert	ihr würdet ärgern
Sie haben geärgert	Sie hatten geärgert	Sie würden ärgern
sie haben geärgert	sie hatten geärgert	sie würden ärgern

SUBJUNCTIVE

INFINITIVE

PRESENT	PERFECT
ich ärgere	ich habe geärgert
du ärgerest	du habest geärgert
er/sie ärgere	er/sie habe geärgert
wir ärgeren	wir haben geärgert
ihr ärgeret	ihr habet geärgert
Sie ärgeren	Sie haben geärgert
sie ärgeren	sie haben geärgert

PRESENT
ärgern
PAST
geärgert haben

PARTICIPLE

IMPERFECT	PLUPERFECT
ich ärgerte	ich hätte geärgert
du ärgertest	du hättest geärgert
er/sie ärgerte	er/sie hätte geärgert
wir ärgerten	wir hätten geärgert
ihr ärgertet	ihr hättet geärgert
Sie ärgerten	Sie hätten geärgert
sie ärgerten	sie hätten geärgert

PRESENT
ärgernd
PAST
geärgert

IMPERATIVE

ärg(e)re!
ärgert!
ärgern Sie!
ärgern wir!

FUTURE PERFECT
ich werde geärgert haben
du wirst geärgert haben *etc*

SICH BEEILEN *to hurry, rush*

PRESENT	**IMPERFECT**	**FUTURE**
ich beeile mich	ich beeilte mich	ich werde mich beeilen
du beeilst dich	du beeiltest dich	du wirst dich beeilen
er/sie beeilt sich	er/sie beeilte sich	er/sie wird sich beeilen
wir beeilen uns	wir beeilten uns	wir werden uns beeilen
ihr beeilt euch	ihr beeiltet euch	ihr werdet euch beeilen
Sie beeilen sich	Sie beeilten sich	Sie werden sich beeilen
sie beeilen sich	sie beeilten sich	sie werden sich beeilen

PERFECT	**PLUPERFECT**	**CONDITIONAL**
ich habe mich beeilt	ich hatte mich beeilt	ich würde mich beeilen
du hast dich beeilt	du hattest dich beeilt	du würdest dich beeilen
er/sie hat sich beeilt	er/sie hatte sich beeilt	er/sie würde sich beeilen
wir haben uns beeilt	wir hatten uns beeilt	wir würden uns beeilen
ihr habt euch beeilt	ihr hattet euch beeilt	ihr würdet euch beeilen
Sie haben sich beeilt	Sie hatten sich beeilt	Sie würden sich beeilen
sie haben sich beeilt	sie hatten sich beeilt	sie würden sich beeilen

SUBJUNCTIVE

PRESENT	**PERFECT**
ich beeile mich	ich habe mich beeilt
du beeilest dich	du habest dich beeilt
er/sie beeile sich	er/sie habe sich beeilt
wir beeilen uns	wir haben uns beeilt
ihr beeilet euch	ihr habet euch beeilt
Sie beeilen sich	Sie haben sich beeilt
sie beeilen sich	sie haben sich beeilt

IMPERFECT	**PLUPERFECT**
ich beeilte mich	ich hätte mich beeilt
du beeiltest dich	du hättest dich beeilt
er/sie beeilte sich	er/sie hätte sich beeilt
wir beeilten uns	wir hätten uns beeilt
ihr beeiltet euch	ihr hättet euch beeilt
Sie beeilten sich	Sie hätten sich beeilt
sie beeilten sich	sie hätten sich beeilt

FUTURE PERFECT
ich werde mich beeilt haben
du wirst dich beeilt haben *etc*

INFINITIVE

PRESENT
sich beeilen
PAST
sich beeilt haben

PARTICIPLE

PRESENT
mich/sich *etc* beeilend

IMPERATIVE

beeile dich!
beeilt euch!
beeilen Sie sich!
beeilen wir uns!

BRAUCHEN *to need*

PRESENT
ich brauche
du brauchst
er/sie braucht
wir brauchen
ihr braucht
Sie brauchen
sie brauchen

IMPERFECT
ich brauchte
du brauchtest
er/sie brauchte
wir brauchten
ihr brauchtet
Sie brauchten
sie brauchten

FUTURE
ich werde brauchen
du wirst brauchen
er/sie wird brauchen
wir werden brauchen
ihr werdet brauchen
Sie werden brauchen
sie werden brauchen

PERFECT
ich habe gebraucht
du hast gebraucht
er/sie hat gebraucht
wir haben gebraucht
ihr habt gebraucht
Sie haben gebraucht
sie haben gebraucht

PLUPERFECT
ich hatte gebraucht
du hattest gebraucht
er/sie hatte gebraucht
wir hatten gebraucht
ihr hattet gebraucht
Sie hatten gebraucht
sie hatten gebraucht

CONDITIONAL
ich würde brauchen
du würdest brauchen
er/sie würde brauchen
wir würden brauchen
ihr würdet brauchen
Sie würden brauchen
sie würden brauchen

SUBJUNCTIVE

PRESENT
ich brauche
du brauchest
er/sie brauche
wir brauchen
ihr brauchet
Sie brauchen
sie brauchen

PERFECT
ich habe gebraucht
du habest gebraucht
er/sie habe gebraucht
wir haben gebraucht
ihr habet gebraucht
Sie haben gebraucht
sie haben gebraucht

INFINITIVE

PRESENT
brauchen
PAST
gebraucht haben

PARTICIPLE

PRESENT
brauchend
PAST
gebraucht

IMPERFECT
ich brauchte
du brauchtest
er/sie brauchte
wir brauchten
ihr brauchtet
Sie brauchten
sie brauchten

PLUPERFECT
ich hätte gebraucht
du hättest gebraucht
er/sie hätte gebraucht
wir hätten gebraucht
ihr hättet gebraucht
Sie hätten gebraucht
sie hätten gebraucht

IMPERATIVE

brauch(e)!
braucht!
brauchen Sie!
brauchen wir!

FUTURE PERFECT
ich werde gebraucht haben
du wirst gebraucht haben *etc*

DÜRFEN *to be allowed to*

PRESENT	**IMPERFECT**	**FUTURE**
ich darf	ich durfte	ich werde dürfen
du darfst	du durftest	du wirst dürfen
er/sie darf	er/sie durfte	er/sie wird dürfen
wir dürfen	wir durften	wir werden dürfen
ihr dürft	ihr durftet	ihr werdet dürfen
Sie dürfen	Sie durften	Sie werden dürfen
sie dürfen	sie durften	sie werden dürfen
PERFECT *(1)*	**PLUPERFECT** *(2)*	**CONDITIONAL**
ich habe gedurft	ich hatte gedurft	ich würde dürfen
du hast gedurft	du hattest gedurft	du würdest dürfen
er/sie hat gedurft	er/sie hatte gedurft	er/sie würde dürfen
wir haben gedurft	wir hatten gedurft	wir würden dürfen
ihr habt gedurft	ihr hattet gedurft	ihr würdet dürfen
Sie haben gedurft	Sie hatten gedurft	Sie würden dürfen
sie haben gedurft	sie hatten gedurft	sie würden dürfen

SUBJUNCTIVE

INFINITIVE

PRESENT	**PERFECT** *(1)*
ich dürfe	ich habe gedurft
du dürfest	du habest gedurft
er/sie dürfe	er/sie habe gedurft
wir dürfen	wir haben gedurft
ihr dürfet	ihr habet gedurft
Sie dürfen	Sie haben gedurft
sie dürfen	sie haben gedurft

PRESENT
dürfen
PAST
gedurft haben

PARTICIPLE

IMPERFECT	**PLUPERFECT** *(3)*
ich dürfte	ich hätte gedurft
du dürftest	du hättest gedurft
er/sie dürfte	er/sie hätte gedurft
wir dürften	wir hätten gedurft
ihr dürftet	ihr hättet gedurft
Sie dürften	Sie hätten gedurft
sie dürften	sie hätten gedurft

PRESENT
dürfend
PAST
gedurft

NOTE when preceded by an infinitive: *(1)* ich habe ... dürfen *etc* *(2)* ich hatte ... dürfen *etc* *(3)* ich hätte ... dürfen *etc*

HABEN *to have*

PRESENT	**IMPERFECT**	**FUTURE**
ich habe	ich hatte	ich werde haben
du hast	du hattest	du wirst haben
er/sie hat	er/sie hatte	er/sie wird haben
wir haben	wir hatten	wir werden haben
ihr habt	ihr hattet	ihr werdet haben
Sie haben	Sie hatten	Sie werden haben
sie haben	sie hatten	sie werden haben

PERFECT	**PLUPERFECT**	**CONDITIONAL**
ich habe gehabt	ich hatte gehabt	ich würde haben
du hast gehabt	du hattest gehabt	du würdest haben
er/sie hat gehabt	er/sie hatte gehabt	er/sie würde haben
wir haben gehabt	wir hatten gehabt	wir würden haben
ihr habt gehabt	ihr hattet gehabt	ihr würdet haben
Sie haben gehabt	Sie hatten gehabt	Sie würden haben
sie haben gehabt	sie hatten gehabt	sie würden haben

SUBJUNCTIVE

PRESENT	**PERFECT**
ich habe	ich habe gehabt
du habest	du habest gehabt
er/sie habe	er/sie habe gehabt
wir haben	wir haben gehabt
ihr habet	ihr habet gehabt
Sie haben	Sie haben gehabt
sie haben	sie haben gehabt

IMPERFECT	**PLUPERFECT**
ich hätte	ich hätte gehabt
du hättest	du hättest gehabt
er/sie hätte	er/sie hätte gehabt
wir hätten	wir hätten gehabt
ihr hättet	ihr hättet gehabt
Sie hätten	Sie hätten gehabt
sie hätten	sie hätten gehabt

FUTURE PERFECT
ich werde gehabt haben
du wirst gehabt haben *etc*

INFINITIVE

PRESENT
haben

PAST
gehabt haben

PARTICIPLE

PRESENT
habend

PAST
gehabt

IMPERATIVE

hab(e)!
habt!
haben Sie!
haben wir!

KÖNNEN *to be able to*

PRESENT	IMPERFECT	FUTURE
ich kann	ich konnte	ich werde können
du kannst	du konntest	du wirst können
er/sie kann	er/sie konnte	er/sie wird können
wir können	wir konnten	wir werden können
ihr könnt	ihr konntet	ihr werdet können
Sie können	Sie konnten	Sie werden können
sie können	sie konnten	sie werden können
PERFECT *(1)*	**PLUPERFECT** *(2)*	**CONDITIONAL**
ich habe gekonnt	ich hatte gekonnt	ich würde können
du hast gekonnt	du hattest gekonnt	du würdest können
er/sie hat gekonnt	er/sie hatte gekonnt	er/sie würde können
wir haben gekonnt	wir hatten gekonnt	wir würden können
ihr habt gekonnt	ihr hattet gekonnt	ihr würdet können
Sie haben gekonnt	Sie hatten gekonnt	Sie würden können
sie haben gekonnt	sie hatten gekonnt	sie würden können

SUBJUNCTIVE

PRESENT	PERFECT *(1)*
ich könne	ich habe gekonnt
du könnest	du habest gekonnt
er/sie könne	er/sie habe gekonnt
wir können	wir haben gekonnt
ihr könnet	ihr habet gekonnt
Sie können	Sie haben gekonnt
sie können	sie haben gekonnt
IMPERFECT	**PLUPERFECT** *(3)*
ich könnte	ich hätte gekonnt
du könntest	du hättest gekonnt
er/sie könnte	er/sie hätte gekonnt
wir könnten	wir hätten gekonnt
ihr könntet	ihr hättet gekonnt
Sie könnten	Sie hätten gekonnt
sie könnten	sie hätten gekonnt

INFINITIVE

PRESENT
können

PAST
gekonnt haben

PARTICIPLE

PRESENT
könnend

PAST
gekonnt

NOTE when preceded by an infinitive: (1) ich habe ... können etc (2) ich hatte ... können etc (3) ich hätte ... können etc

MÖGEN *to like*

PRESENT	IMPERFECT	FUTURE
ich mag	ich mochte	ich werde mögen
du magst	du mochtest	du wirst mögen
er/sie mag	er/sie mochte	er/sie wird mögen
wir mögen	wir mochten	wir werden mögen
ihr mögt	ihr mochtet	ihr werdet mögen
Sie mögen	Sie mochten	Sie werden mögen
sie mögen	sie mochten	sie werden mögen
PERFECT *(1)*	PLUPERFECT *(2)*	CONDITIONAL
ich habe gemocht	ich hatte gemocht	ich würde mögen
du hast gemocht	du hattest gemocht	du würdest mögen
er/sie hat gemocht	er/sie hatte gemocht	er/sie würde mögen
wir haben gemocht	wir hatten gemocht	wir würden mögen
ihr habt gemocht	ihr hattet gemocht	ihr würdet mögen
Sie haben gemocht	Sie hatten gemocht	Sie würden mögen
sie haben gemocht	sie hatten gemocht	sie würden mögen

SUBJUNCTIVE

PRESENT	PERFECT *(1)*
ich möge	ich habe gemocht
du mögest	du habest gemocht
er/sie möge	er/sie habe gemocht
wir mögen	wir haben gemocht
ihr möget	ihr habet gemocht
Sie mögen	Sie haben gemocht
sie mögen	sie haben gemocht
IMPERFECT	PLUPERFECT *(3)*
ich möchte	ich hätte gemocht
du möchtest	du hättest gemocht
er/sie möchte	er/sie hätte gemocht
wir möchten	wir hätten gemocht
ihr möchtet	ihr hättet gemocht
Sie möchten	Sie hätten gemocht
sie möchten	sie hätten gemocht

INFINITIVE

PRESENT
mögen
PAST
gemocht haben

PARTICIPLE

PRESENT
mögend
PAST
gemocht

NOTE when preceded by an infinitive: (1) ich habe ... mögen *etc (2)* ich hatte ... mögen *etc (3)* ich hätte ... mögen *etc*

MÜSSEN *to have to*

PRESENT	IMPERFECT	FUTURE
ich muss	ich musste	ich werde müssen
du musst	du musstest	du wirst müssen
er/sie muss	er/sie musste	er/sie wird müssen
wir müssen	wir mussten	wir werden müssen
ihr müsst	ihr musstet	ihr werdet müssen
Sie müssen	Sie mussten	Sie werden müssen
sie müssen	sie mussten	sie werden müssen
PERFECT *(1)*	**PLUPERFECT** *(2)*	**CONDITIONAL**
ich habe gemusst	ich hatte gemusst	ich würde müssen
du hast gemusst	du hattest gemusst	du würdest müssen
er/sie hat gemusst	er/sie hatte gemusst	er/sie würde müssen
wir haben gemusst	wir hatten gemusst	wir würden müssen
ihr habt gemusst	ihr hattet gemusst	ihr würdet müssen
Sie haben gemusst	Sie hatten gemusst	Sie würden müssen
sie haben gemusst	sie hatten gemusst	sie würden müssen

SUBJUNCTIVE

INFINITIVE

PRESENT	PERFECT *(1)*	PRESENT
ich müsse	ich habe gemusst	müssen
du müssest	du habest gemusst	**PAST**
er/sie müsse	er/sie habe gemusst	gemusst haben
wir müssen	wir haben gemusst	
ihr müsset	ihr habet gemusst	**PARTICIPLE**
Sie müssen	Sie haben gemusst	
sie müssen	sie haben gemusst	PRESENT
IMPERFECT	**PLUPERFECT** *(3)*	müssend
ich müsste	ich hätte gemusst	**PAST**
du müsstest	du hättest gemusst	gemusst
er/sie müsste	er/sie hätte gemusst	
wir müssten	wir hätten gemusst	
ihr müsstet	ihr hättet gemusst	
Sie müssten	Sie hätten gemusst	
sie müssten	sie hätten gemusst	

NOTE when preceded by an infinitive: (1) ich habe ... müssen etc (2) ich hatte ... müssen etc (3) ich hätte ... müssen etc

PASSEN *to fit, suit*

PRESENT
ich passe
du passt
er/sie passt
wir passen
ihr passt
Sie passen
sie passen

PERFECT
ich habe gepasst
du hast gepasst
er/sie hat gepasst
wir haben gepasst
ihr habt gepasst
Sie haben gepasst
sie haben gepasst

IMPERFECT
ich passte
du passtest
er/sie passte
wir passten
ihr passtet
Sie passten
sie passten

PLUPERFECT
ich hatte gepasst
du hattest gepasst
er/sie hatte gepasst
wir hatten gepasst
ihr hattet gepasst
Sie hatten gepasst
sie hatten gepasst

FUTURE
ich werde passen
du wirst passen
er/sie wird passen
wir werden passen
ihr werdet passen
Sie werden passen
sie werden passen

CONDITIONAL
ich würde passen
du würdest passen
er/sie würde passen
wir würden passen
ihr würdet passen
Sie würden passen
sie würden passen

SUBJUNCTIVE

PRESENT
ich passe
du passest
er/sie passe
wir passen
ihr passet
Sie passen
sie passen

IMPERFECT
ich passte
du passtest
er/sie passte
wir passten
ihr passtet
Sie passten
sie passten

FUTURE PERFECT
ich werde gepasst haben
du wirst gepasst haben *etc*

PERFECT
ich habe gepasst
du habest gepasst
er/sie habe gepasst
wir haben gepasst
ihr habet gepasst
Sie haben gepasst
sie haben gepasst

PLUPERFECT
ich hätte gepasst
du hättest gepasst
er/sie hätte gepasst
wir hätten gepasst
ihr hättet gepasst
Sie hätten gepasst
sie hätten gepasst

INFINITIVE

PRESENT
passen
PAST
gepasst haben

PARTICIPLE

PRESENT
passend
PAST
gepasst

IMPERATIVE

pass! passe!
passt!
passen Sie!
passen wir!

SEIN *to be*

PRESENT	**IMPERFECT**	**FUTURE**
ich bin	ich war	ich werde sein
du bist	du warst	du wirst sein
er/sie ist	er/sie war	er/sie wird sein
wir sind	wir waren	wir werden sein
ihr seid	ihr wart	ihr werdet sein
Sie sind	Sie waren	Sie werden sein
sie sind	sie waren	sie werden sein
PERFECT	**PLUPERFECT**	**CONDITIONAL**
ich bin gewesen	ich war gewesen	ich würde sein
du bist gewesen	du warst gewesen	du würdest sein
er/sie ist gewesen	er/sie war gewesen	er/sie würde sein
wir sind gewesen	wir waren gewesen	wir würden sein
ihr seid gewesen	ihr wart gewesen	ihr würdet sein
Sie sind gewesen	Sie waren gewesen	Sie würden sein
sie sind gewesen	sie waren gewesen	sie würden sein

SUBJUNCTIVE

PRESENT	**PERFECT**
ich sei	ich sei gewesen
du sei(e)st	du sei(e)st gewesen
er/sie sei	er/sie sei gewesen
wir seien	wir seien gewesen
ihr seiet	ihr seiet gewesen
Sie seien	Sie seien gewesen
sie seien	sie seien gewesen
IMPERFECT	**PLUPERFECT**
ich wäre	ich wäre gewesen
du wär(e)st	du wär(e)st gewesen
er/sie wäre	er/sie wäre gewesen
wir wären	wir wären gewesen
ihr wär(e)t	ihr wär(e)t gewesen
Sie wären	Sie wären gewesen
sie wären	sie wären gewesen

FUTURE PERFECT
ich werde gewesen sein
du wirst gewesen sein *etc*

INFINITIVE

PRESENT
sein
PAST
gewesen sein

PARTICIPLE

PRESENT
seiend
PAST
gewesen

IMPERATIVE

sei!
seid!
seien Sie!
seien wir!

SOLLEN *to be supposed to*

PRESENT	IMPERFECT	FUTURE
ich soll	ich sollte	ich werde sollen
du sollst	du solltest	du wirst sollen
er/sie soll	er/sie sollte	er/sie wird sollen
wir sollen	wir sollten	wir werden sollen
ihr sollt	ihr solltet	ihr werdet sollen
Sie sollen	Sie sollten	Sie werden sollen
sie sollen	sie sollten	sie werden sollen

PERFECT *(1)*	PLUPERFECT *(2)*	CONDITIONAL
ich habe gesollt	ich hatte gesollt	ich würde sollen
du hast gesollt	du hattest gesollt	du würdest sollen
er/sie hat gesollt	er/sie hatte gesollt	er/sie würde sollen
wir haben gesollt	wir hatten gesollt	wir würden sollen
ihr habt gesollt	ihr hattet gesollt	ihr würdet sollen
Sie haben gesollt	Sie hatten gesollt	Sie würden sollen
sie haben gesollt	sie hatten gesollt	sie würden sollen

SUBJUNCTIVE

PRESENT	PERFECT *(1)*
ich solle	ich habe gesollt
du sollest	du habest gesollt
er/sie solle	er/sie habe gesollt
wir sollen	wir haben gesollt
ihr sollet	ihr habet gesollt
Sie sollen	Sie haben gesollt
sie sollen	sie haben gesollt

IMPERFECT	PLUPERFECT *(3)*
ich sollte	ich hätte gesollt
du solltest	du hättest gesollt
er/sie sollte	er/sie hätte gesollt
wir sollten	wir hätten gesollt
ihr solltet	ihr hättet gesollt
Sie sollten	Sie hätten gesollt
sie sollten	sie hätten gesollt

INFINITIVE

PRESENT
sollen

PAST
gesollt haben

PARTICIPLE

PRESENT
sollend

PAST
gesollt

> *NOTE when preceded by an infinitive: (1) ich habe ... sollen etc (2) ich hatte ... sollen etc (3) ich hätte ... sollen etc*

191

STÜRZEN *to fall, plunge, rush*

PRESENT	**IMPERFECT**	**FUTURE**
ich stürze	ich stürzte	ich werde stürzen
du stürzt	du stürztest	du wirst stürzen
er/sie stürzt	er/sie stürzte	er/sie wird stürzen
wir stürzen	wir stürzten	wir werden stürzen
ihr stürzt	ihr stürztet	ihr werdet stürzen
Sie stürzen	Sie stürzten	Sie werden stürzen
sie stürzen	sie stürzten	sie werden stürzen

PERFECT	**PLUPERFECT**	**CONDITIONAL**
ich bin gestürzt	ich war gestürzt	ich würde stürzen
du bist gestürzt	du warst gestürzt	du würdest stürzen
er/sie ist gestürzt	er/sie war gestürzt	er/sie würde stürzen
wir sind gestürzt	wir waren gestürzt	wir würden stürzen
ihr seid gestürzt	ihr wart gestürzt	ihr würdet stürzen
Sie sind gestürzt	Sie waren gestürzt	Sie würden stürzen
sie sind gestürzt	sie waren gestürzt	sie würden stürzen

SUBJUNCTIVE

PRESENT	**PERFECT**
ich stürze	ich sei gestürzt
du stürzest	du sei(e)st gestürzt
er/sie stürze	er/sie sei gestürzt
wir stürzen	wir seien gestürzt
ihr stürzet	ihr seiet gestürzt
Sie stürzen	Sie seien gestürzt
sie stürzen	sie seien gestürzt

IMPERFECT	**PLUPERFECT**
ich stürzte	ich wäre gestürzt
du stürztest	du wär(e)st gestürzt
er/sie stürzte	er/sie wäre gestürzt
wir stürzten	wir wären gestürzt
ihr stürztet	ihr wär(e)t gestürzt
Sie stürzten	Sie wären gestürzt
sie stürzten	sie wären gestürzt

FUTURE PERFECT
ich werde gestürzt sein
du wirst gestürzt sein *etc*

INFINITIVE

PRESENT
stürzen

PAST
gestürzt sein

PARTICIPLE

PRESENT
stürzend

PAST
gestürzt

IMPERATIVE

stürz(e)!
stürzt!
stürzen Sie!
stürzen wir!

WARTEN *to wait*

PRESENT	IMPERFECT	FUTURE
ich warte	ich wartete	ich werde warten
du wartest	du wartetest	du wirst warten
er/sie wartet	er/sie wartete	er/sie wird warten
wir warten	wir warteten	wir werden warten
ihr wartet	ihr wartetet	ihr werdet warten
Sie warten	Sie warteten	Sie werden warten
sie warten	sie warteten	sie werden warten

PERFECT	PLUPERFECT	CONDITIONAL
ich habe gewartet	ich hatte gewartet	ich würde warten
du hast gewartet	du hattest gewartet	du würdest warten
er/sie hat gewartet	er/sie hatte gewartet	er/sie würde warten
wir haben gewartet	wir hatten gewartet	wir würden warten
ihr habt gewartet	ihr hattet gewartet	ihr würdet warten
Sie haben gewartet	Sie hatten gewartet	Sie würden warten
sie haben gewartet	sie hatten gewartet	sie würden warten

SUBJUNCTIVE

PRESENT	PERFECT
ich warte	ich habe gewartet
du wartest	du habest gewartet
er/sie warte	er/sie habe gewartet
wir warten	wir haben gewartet
ihr wartet	ihr habet gewartet
Sie warten	Sie haben gewartet
sie warten	sie haben gewartet

IMPERFECT	PLUPERFECT
ich wartete	ich hätte gewartet
du wartetest	du hättest gewartet
er/sie wartete	er/sie hätte gewartet
wir warteten	wir hätten gewartet
ihr wartetet	ihr hättet gewartet
Sie warteten	Sie hätten gewartet
sie warteten	sie hätten gewartet

FUTURE PERFECT
ich werde gewartet haben
du wirst gewartet haben *etc*

INFINITIVE

PRESENT
warten
PAST
gewartet haben

PARTICIPLE

PRESENT
wartend
PAST
gewartet

IMPERATIVE

warte(e)!
wartet!
warten Sie!
warten wir!

WERDEN *to become*

PRESENT	IMPERFECT	FUTURE
ich werde	ich wurde	ich werde werden
du wirst	du wurdest	du wirst werden
er/sie wird	er/sie wurde	er/sie wird werden
wir werden	wir wurden	wir werden werden
ihr werdet	ihr wurdet	ihr werdet werden
Sie werden	Sie wurden	Sie werden werden
sie werden	sie wurden	sie werden werden
PERFECT *(1)*	**PLUPERFECT** *(2)*	**CONDITIONAL**
ich bin geworden	ich war geworden	ich würde werden
du bist geworden	du warst geworden	du würdest werden
er/sie ist geworden	er/sie war geworden	er/sie würde werden
wir sind geworden	wir waren geworden	wir würden werden
ihr seid geworden	ihr wart geworden	ihr würdet werden
Sie sind geworden	Sie waren geworden	Sie würden werden
sie sind geworden	sie waren geworden	sie würden werden

SUBJUNCTIVE

PRESENT	PERFECT *(3)*
ich werde	ich sei geworden
du werdest	du sei(e)st geworden
er/sie werde	er/sie sei geworden
wir werden	wir seien geworden
ihr werdet	ihr seiet geworden
Sie werden	Sie seien geworden
sie werden	sie seien geworden

IMPERFECT	PLUPERFECT *(4)*
ich würde	ich wäre geworden
du würdest	du wär(e)st geworden
er/sie würde	er/sie wäre geworden
wir würden	wir wären geworden
ihr würdet	ihr wär(e)t geworden
Sie würden	Sie wären geworden
sie würden	sie wären geworden
FUTURE PERFECT *(5)*	
ich werde geworden sein	
du wirst geworden	
sein *etc*	

INFINITIVE

PRESENT
werden

PAST *(6)*
geworden sein

PARTICIPLE

PRESENT
werdend

PAST
geworden

IMPERATIVE

werde!
werdet!
werden Sie!
werden wir!

NOTE geworden *becomes* worden *when preceded by a past participle to form the passive* : *(1)* ich bin ... worden *etc (2)* ich war ...worden *etc (3)* ich sei ... worden *etc (4)* ich wäre ...worden *etc (5)* ich werde ... worden sein *etc (6)* ...worden sein

WOLLEN *to want (to)*

PRESENT	IMPERFECT	FUTURE
ich will	ich wollte	ich werde wollen
du willst	du wolltest	du wirst wollen
er/sie will	er/sie wollte	er/sie wird wollen
wir wollen	wir wollten	wir werden wollen
ihr wollt	ihr wolltet	ihr werdet wollen
Sie wollen	Sie wollten	Sie werden wollen
sie wollen	sie wollten	sie werden wollen

PERFECT *(1)*	PLUPERFECT *(2)*	CONDITIONAL
ich habe gewollt	ich hatte gewollt	ich würde wollen
du hast gewollt	du hattest gewollt	du würdest wollen
er/sie hat gewollt	er/sie hatte gewollt	er/sie würde wollen
wir haben gewollt	wir hatten gewollt	wir würden wollen
ihr habt gewollt	ihr hattet gewollt	ihr würdet wollen
Sie haben gewollt	Sie hatten gewollt	Sie würden wollen
sie haben gewollt	sie hatten gewollt	sie würden wollen

SUBJUNCTIVE

INFINITIVE

PRESENT	PERFECT *(1)*
ich wolle	ich habe gewollt
du wollest	du habest gewollt
er/sie wolle	er/sie habe gewollt
wir wollen	wir haben gewollt
ihr wollet	ihr habet gewollt
Sie wollen	Sie haben gewollt
sie wollen	sie haben gewollt

PRESENT
wollen
PAST
gewollt haben

PARTICIPLE

PRESENT
wollend

IMPERFECT	PLUPERFECT *(3)*
ich wollte	ich hätte gewollt
du wolltest	du hättest gewollt
er/sie wollte	er/sie hätte gewollt
wir wollten	wir hätten gewollt
ihr wolltet	ihr hättet gewollt
Sie wollten	Sie hätten gewollt
sie wollten	sie hätten gewollt

PAST
gewollt

IMPERATIVE

woll(e)!
wollt!
wollen Sie!
wollen wir!

NOTE: *when preceded by an infinitive: (1)* ich habe ...
wollen *etc (2)* ich hatte ... wollen *etc (3)* ich hätte ...
wollen *etc*

8 PREPOSITIONS

Prepositions are words such as 'from', 'in', 'with'. They are followed by nouns or pronouns, which, in German, must be in the case determined by the preposition. Many take only one case, but some are followed by one of two cases (*see* **sections C and E**).

The most common prepositions are given below in five categories according to whether they take the dative, the accusative, the genitive, the dative or accusative, or the genitive or dative case. They are listed in alphabetical order, with the generally accepted meanings on the left, a description of their use in brackets, and an illustration of their usage.

A WITH THE DATIVE ONLY

AUS

OUT OF	*(place)*	**er lief aus dem Haus**
		he ran out of the house
FROM	*(place)*	**ich stamme aus Italien**
		I come from Italy
	(place)	**aus dieser Richtung**
		from this direction
	(time)	**ein Gemälde aus dem 18. Jahrhundert**
		a painting from the 18th century
	(cause)	**aus Langeweile**
		from boredom
MADE OF	*(material)*	**aus Messing**
		made of brass

AUSSER

APART FROM	**außer einem Frosch habe ich keine Haustiere**
	apart from a frog I don't have any pets

OUT OF		**außer Atem/Betrieb/Gefahr/Kontrolle**
		out of breath/order/danger/control
OUT	*(idiom)*	**wir essen nie außer Hause**
		we never eat out

BEI

NEAR	*(place)*	**er wohnt bei der Post**
		he lives near the post
AT	*(place)*	**bei mir/Ihnen/Schmidts**
		at my/your/the Schmidts' house
		beim Bäcker
		at the baker's
		bei Woolworth
		at Woolworth's
	(time)	**bei Tagesanbruch**
		at daybreak

Note that bei cannot be used with verbs of motion:

er übernachtet bei seiner Mutter
he's spending the night at his mother's

but:

er fährt gerade zu seiner Mutter
he's on his way to his mother's

ON	*(time)*	**bei seiner Ankunft/Abfahrt**
		on his arrival/departure
	(position)	**hat jemand Geld bei sich?**
		has anyone got any money on them?
WITH	*(+ pronoun)*	**bei ihr war es anders**
		with her it was different
IN	*(with writers etc)*	**bei Goethe/Shakespeare**
		in Goethe/Shakespeare
BY	*(time)*	**bei Tag/Nacht**
		by day/night
—	*(+ gerund)*	**er ist gerade beim Abwaschen**
		he's (just) washing up

GEGENÜBER

OPPOSITE/ FACING	*(place)*	**gegenüber dem Park/dem Park gegenüber** opposite the park
TOWARDS	*(relationship)*	**er ist mir gegenüber sehr freundlich** he's very friendly towards me
COMPARED WITH		**ihm gegenüber ist sie fast ein Genie** compared with him she's practically a genius

GEMÄSS

| IN ACCORDANCE WITH | **unseren Wünschen gemäß**
in accordance with our wishes |

MIT

WITH	*(association)*	**mit nur einem Löffel Zucker** with just one spoon of sugar
	(means)	**er geht mit einem Stock** he walks with a stick
		mit ihr ist heute nichts anzufangen you won't get anywhere with her today
BY	*(means)*	**mit dem Auto/Flugzeug/Zug** by car/plane/train
IN	*(time)*	**mit der Zeit** in (the course of) time
AT	*(time)*	**mit 30 Jahren** at 30 (years of age)
	(speed)	**mit 100 Stundenkilometern** at 100 kilometres an hour

NACH

TO	*(place)*	**der Zug nach Athen**
		the train to Athens
	(place)	**wer geht nach Hause?**
		who's going home?
	(place)	**nach rechts/links/oben/unten gehen**
		to go right/left/upstairs/downstairs
AFTER	*(time)*	**nach der Prüfung/zwei Jahren**
		after the exam/two years
PAST	*(time)*	**es ist 5 (Minuten) nach 3**
		it's 5 (minutes) past 3
		meiner/Ihrer Meinung nach
		in my/your opinion

VON

FROM	*(place)*	**von Lübeck bis Hamburg**
		from Lübeck to Hamburg
		von dieser Stelle aus kann man die Berge sehen
		from this position you can see the mountains
		wir holen dich vom (= von dem) Bahnhof ab
		we'll collect you from the station
FROM	*(time)*	**von 6 bis 9 Uhr abends**
		from 6 to 9 in the evening
		vom 1. bis zum 15. Juli
		from the 1st to the 15th of July
OF	*(possession)*	**ein Freund von mir**
		a friend of mine
		jeder/viele von uns
		each/many of us

Note that in colloquial language, von is often used instead of the genitive case:

die Erwartungen von deutschen Teenagern (= deutscher Teenager)
the expectations of German teenagers

PREPOSITIONS

BY	*(agent)*	**dieses Dorf wurde vom Feind zerstört** this village was destroyed by the enemy **eine Platte von den Beatles** a record by the Beatles
ZU		
TO	*(place)*	**bitte, komm zu mir!** come to me, please! **wie komme ich zur (= zu der) Post?** how do I get to the post office? **er muss zum (= zu dem) Arzt** he has to go to the doctor's
AT	*(place)*	**zu Hause sein** to be at home
	(time)	**zu Ostern/Weihnachten** at Easter/Christmas **zurzeit** at present
	(price)	**zu 30 Euro das Stück** at 30 euros each **zum halben Preis** at half price
FOR	*(time)*	**zum ersten Mal** for the first time
ON	*(manner)*	**zu Fuß** on foot
—	*(+ gerund)*	**sie kam kaum zum Schreiben** she hardly got round to writing

B **WITH THE ACCUSATIVE ONLY**

BIS

TILL	*(time)*	**bis nächstes Jahr!**
		till next year!

Note that 'not till' is translated by erst:

ich fahre erst morgen in Urlaub
I'm not going on holiday till tomorrow

	(idiom)	**bis bald/später!**
		see you soon/later!
BY	*(time)*	**bis morgen**
		by tomorrow

Note that bis is often coupled with other prepositions, which then determine the case of the following noun or pronoun:

bis zum 10. Juni
by the 10th of June
bis an die Grenze
as far as the border

but:

bis München
as far as Munich

bis auf dich sind wir alle fertig
we're all ready except for you

DURCH

THROUGH	*(place)*	**er rannte durch das Dorf**
		he ran through the village
	(agent)	**ich habe sie durch meinen Vater kennengelernt**
		I got to know her through my father
	(means)	**nur durch Fleiß macht man Fortschritte**
		only through hard work do you make progress
BY	*(passive)*	**durch Zufall**
		by chance
		die Ernte wurde durch Hagel vernichtet
		the harvest was destroyed by hail

ENTLANG

(usually with accusative)

| ALONG | *(place)* | **sie rannte die Straße entlang** |
| | | she ran along the street |

FÜR

FOR	*(person)*	**ich habe ein Geschenk für dich!**
		I have a present for you!
	(time)	**sie ging für ein Jahr ins Ausland**
		she went abroad for a year
	(price)	**wir haben es für 500 Euro bekommen**
		we bought it for 500 euros

GEGEN

AGAINST	*(place)*	**er lehnte sich gegen die Mauer**
		he leant against the wall
		was hast du gegen mich/diese Idee?
		what have you got against me/this idea?
ABOUT	*(time)*	**gegen 6 Uhr**
		about 6 o'clock
TOWARDS	*(time)*	**gegen Abend/Ende des Monats**
		towards evening/the end of the month
IN RETURN FOR		**gegen Quittung bekommen Sie Ihr Geld zurück**
		you'll get your money back in return for your receipt
CONTRARY TO		**gegen alle Erwartungen**
		contrary to all expectations
FOR		**haben Sie Tabletten gegen Halsweh?**
		do you have any tablets for a sore throat?

OHNE

| WITHOUT | | **sie kam ohne ihre Eltern** |
| | | she came without her parents |

PER

(usually without a following article)

BY		**per Post**
		by post
–	*(idiom)*	**ich bin per du mit ihr**
		I'm on first name terms with her

PRO

(usually without a following article)

zwei Mal pro Tag	**50 Euro pro Stück**
twice a day	50 euros each

UM

ROUND	*(place)*	**er fährt gerade um die Ecke**
		he's just driving round the corner
	(place)	**wir alle standen um sie (herum)**
		we all stood round her
AT	*(time)*	**um 11 Uhr**
		at 11 o'clock
AROUND	*(time)*	**diese Kirche wurde um 1400 gebaut**
		this church was built around 1400
BY	*(amount)*	**um fünf Euro billiger**
		cheaper by five euros

C WITH THE DATIVE OR ACCUSATIVE

1 A number of German prepositions are followed by either
the dative or accusative case. The most common are:

an	on(to), against, to, at, in
auf	(down) on(to)
hinter	behind
in	in(to)

neben	next to, beside
über	above, over
unter	under(neath), below
vor	in front of, before
zwischen	between

As a general rule, the dative is used where the position or location of a person, thing or action is signified. wo? is thus the question word most likely to prompt a statement of this kind.

wo ist Katrin?	→	**sie sitzt auf dem Sofa**
where is Katrin?		she's sitting on the sofa
wo hängt der Spiegel?	→	**er hängt an der Tür**
where's the mirror (hanging)?		it's (hanging) on the door
wo kann man hier einen Spaziergang machen?	→	**im Park kann man einen Spaziergang machen**
where can you go for a walk here?		you can go for a walk in the park

The accusative indicates movement to, or in the direction of, a new position. wohin? is therefore the question word most likely to elicit a statement of this kind.

wohin fließt der Fluss?	→	**er fließt in den Bodensee**
where does the river flow to?		it flows into Lake Constance
wohin ist die Katze gesprungen?	→	**sie ist auf den Kühlschrank gesprungen**
where did the cat jump to?		it jumped onto the fridge

The following short forms are very common, both in spoken and written German:

ans (= an das)	am (= an dem)
ins (= in das)	im (= in dem)

Other examples of abbreviation:

aufs (= auf das)	auf'm (= auf dem) *(used only in colloquial speech)*
hinters (= hinter das)	hinterm (= hinter dem)
übers (= über das)	überm (= über dem)
unters (= unter das)	unterm (= unter dem)
vors (= vor das)	vorm (= vor dem)

Note that there are no standard short forms with neben and zwischen, although in colloquial German, nebens (= neben das) is possible.

For the combination of prepositions with pronouns (darin, darauf, etc) *see* p 91.

2 The following examples begin in each case with a pair of sentences to make clear the essential difference between these prepositions in their accusative and dative use:

AN

ACCUSATIVE	DATIVE
sie klebte das Foto an die Tür	**das Foto klebt an der Tür**
she stuck the photo on the door	the photo is stuck on the door
wir fliegen jeden Sommer ans Mittelmeer	**normalerweise zelten wir am Mittelmeer**
every summer we fly to the Mediterranean	we normally camp on the Mediterranean

ON *(time)*	**am Sonntag**	
	on Sunday	
	am 31. August	
	on the 31st of August	
IN *(time)*	**am Morgen/Abend**	
	in the morning/evening	
(idiom)	**an Ihrer Stelle**	
	in your position	
AT *(time)*	**am Wochenende**	
	at the weekend	
(place)	**an einer Schule/Universität**	
	at a school/university	

AUF

ACCUSATIVE		**DATIVE**	
stellen Sie bitte Ihr Gepäck nicht auf das Bett!		mein Koffer steht aber nicht auf dem Bett	
please don't put your luggage on the bed		but my suitcase isn't on the bed	
sie ist gerade auf ihr Zimmer gegangen		auf ihrem Zimmer schläft sie sicher bald ein	
she's just gone to her room		she'll soon fall asleep in her room	
TO *(place)*	auf den Markt gehen	AT *(place)*	auf dem Markt sein
	to go to the market		to be at the market
	er zieht aufs Land	IN *(place)*	er wohnt auf dem Lande
	he's moving to the country(side)		he lives in the country(side)
			auf einem Bild/der Welt
			in a picture/the world
IN *(manner)*	auf diese Weise		
	in this way		
(language)	auf Deutsch		
	in German		
FOR *(time)*	auf einige Tage		
	for a few days		
		FROM *(place)*	auf 3 Kilometer zu sehen/hören
			visible/audible from 3 kilometres
	auf jeden Fall		
	whatever happens		
	auf einen Baum klettern		
	to climb a tree		

HINTER

ACCUSATIVE

geh nicht hinter das Haus!
don't go behind the house!

bitte setzen Sie sich hinter mich!
please sit behind me

DATIVE

ein Teich liegt hinter dem Haus
there's a pond behind the house

nun sitzen alle hinter mir
now everyone's sitting behind me

AFTER *(place)*	**die erste Station hinter Stuttgart** the first stop after Stuttgart
(chasing)	**die Behörden sind hinter ihnen her** the authorities are after them
BEYOND *(place)*	**einige Kilometer hinter der Grenze** a few kilometres beyond the border

IN

ACCUSATIVE

unsere Katze kommt gern in die Küche
our cat likes coming into the kitchen

er geht in die Kirche/ins Kino/in den Zoo
he's going to church/to the cinema/the zoo

DATIVE

unsere Katze schläft gern in der Küche
our cat likes sleeping in the kitchen

er ist in der Kirche/im Kino/im Zoo
he's in church/at the cinema/the zoo

TO *(place)*	**in die Alpen/die USA/ ins Ausland reisen** to travel to the Alps/ the USA/abroad	IN *(place)*	**in den Alpen/den USA/ im Ausland arbeiten** to work in the Alps/the USA/abroad

Note the following points:

With most countries the relevant prepositions are nach and in:

nach Schweden reisen to travel to Sweden	**in Schweden arbeiten** to work in Sweden

Compare 'I've never been to France/Switzerland' and ich war noch nie in Frankreich/in der Schweiz

	in Urlaub fahren/ gehen to go on holiday	**im Urlaub sein** to be on holiday
IN *(place)*	**gehen Sie in diese Richtung!** go in this direction	**gehen Sie in dieser Richtung weiter!** keep going in this direction

Note the following:

wir fahren jetzt Richtung Moskau
we're travelling now in the direction of Moscow

schreib ihre Adresse in dein Notizbuch!
write her address (down) in your notebook

IN *(clothes)*	**in einen blauen Anzug gekleidet** dressed in a blue suit		**in Stiefeln/Blau gehen** to wear boots/blue
INTO *(time)*	**es dauert bis spät in die Nacht (hinein)** it goes on (well) into the night		
		IN *(time)*	**in einer Minute** in one minute

		in der Nacht
		in the night
		im November/Herbst
		in November/autumn
		im Jahre 1967
		in 1967
IN		**im Vorbeigehen**
(+ gerund)		**lächelte sie mich an**
		she smiled at me in
		passing
AT *(activity)*		**gut in Physik**
		good at physics
ON *(idioms)*		**im Durchschnitt**
		on average
		im Gegenteil
		on the contrary
		im Ganzen
		on the whole

NEBEN

ACCUSATIVE

sie setzte sich neben mich
she sat down beside me

DATIVE

sie saß neben mir
she was sitting beside me
er ging neben mir her
he walked beside me
compare with:
**neben meinen Schuhen sind deine
sehr billig**
compared with my shoes yours are
very cheap

IN ADDI-
TION TO   **neben diesen Kosten
muss ich noch
Mehrwertsteuer
zahlen**
in addition to these costs
I also have to pay VAT

ÜBER

ACCUSATIVE	DATIVE
fahren Sie links über den Kanal	**über dem Kanal lag dichter Nebel**
go left over the canal	there was a thick fog over the canal
ein Panzerwagen fährt über das Feld	**ein Hubschrauber kreiste über dem Haus**
a tank is driving across the field	a helicopter was circling over the house

VIA *(place)*	**wir fliegen über die Türkei nach Moskau**
	we're flying to Moscow via Turkey
THROUGH *(agent)*	**das habe ich über einen Freund bekommen**
	I got it through a friend

OVER *(seniority)*	**sie steht über uns allen**
	she is over us all
but:	**seit über einem Jahr wohne ich hier**
	I've lived here for over a year

OVER *(time)*	**über eine Stunde**
	over (= more than) an hour

	übers Wochenende
	over the weekend
	das ganze Jahr über
	all year round
ON/ ABOUT	**ein Buch über die deutsche Grammatik**
	a book on German grammar
FOR	**ein Scheck über 100 Euro**
	a cheque for 100 euros

ABOVE	**über dem Durchschnitt**
	above average

UNTER

ACCUSATIVE

das Flugzeug flog unter die Brücke
the plane flew under(neath) the bridge

er legte sich unter den Baum
he lay down underneath the tree

DATIVE

ich warte schon eine Stunde unter dieser Brücke
I've been waiting for an hour under this bridge

die Kinder spielten unter dem Baum
the children were playing under the tree

UNDER *(seniority)*	**Sie haben 2 Arbeiter unter sich** you have 2 workers under you
UNDER *(time)*	**Kinder unter 10 Jahren** children under 10 (years of age)
IN *(idiom)*	**unter Umständen** in certain circumstances
UNDER *(less than)*	**unter einem Kilo/Euro** under a kilo/one euro
BELOW	**unter dem Meeresspiegel** below sea level **unter dem Durchschnitt** below average
AMONG	**unter ihren Freunden** among her friends **unter anderem** among other things
ON *(idiom)*	**unter der Bedingung, dass ...** on condition that ...

BY	**was versteht man unter Onlinewerbung?**
	what do you understand by 'online advertising'?

VOR

ACCUSATIVE	**DATIVE**
er setzt sich sofort vor den Fernseher	**er sitzt den ganzen Abend vor dem Fernseher**
he immediately sits (down) in front of the television	he sits all evening in front of the television

		vor ihm lag nichts als Schlamm
		ahead of him lay nothing but mud
BEFORE	*(order)*	**A kommt vor B**
		A comes before B
BEFORE	*(time)*	**vor dem Krieg**
		before the war
		vor dem 19. November
		before the 19th of November
AGO	*(time)*	**vor einem Jahr/einiger Zeit**
		a year/some time ago
TO	*(time)*	**20 (Minuten) vor 6**
		20 (minutes) to 6
OF	*(cause)*	**vor Hunger/Langeweile sterben**
		to die of hunger/boredom
WITH	*(cause)*	**vor Kälte zittern**
		to shiver with cold
		grün vor Neid
		green with envy
ABOVE	*(idiom)*	**vor allem/allen Dingen**
		above all

TO   **er murmelte vor sich hin**
(idiom)   he was mumbling to
            himself

ZWISCHEN

ACCUSATIVE	**DATIVE**
der Turm fiel zwischen zwei große Lastwagen	**der Turm zwischen den jungen Bäumen steht noch**
the tower fell between two big lorries	the tower between the young trees is still standing

BETWEEN   **zwischen 4 und 5 Uhr**
(time)   between 4 and 5 o'clock
            **Kinder zwischen 5 und
            10 Jahren**
            children between 5 and
            10 (years of age)

Note the following:

> **er ist zwischen 50 und 60 Jahre alt**
> he's between 50 and 60 (years old)

(quantity)   **zwischen 10 und
                12 Euro pro Stunde**
                between 10 and
                12 euros an hour
                **was ist der Unterschied
                zwischen Butter und
                Margarine?**
                what's the difference
                between butter and
                margarine?

 D WITH THE GENITIVE

ANHAND
BY MEANS OF   **er erläuterte seine Theorie anhand eines
                           Beispiels**
                           he explained his theory by means of an
                           example

PREPOSITIONS

AUSSERHALB

OUTSIDE	*(place)*	**eine Kirche steht außerhalb des Dorf(e)s**
		there's a church outside the village
	(time)	**außerhalb der Arbeitszeit**
		outside working hours

DIESSEITS

| ON THIS SIDE OF | *(place)* | **diesseits der Straße** |
| | | on this side of the street |

INNERHALB

INSIDE	*(place)*	**innerhalb der Raumkapsel**
		inside the space capsule
WITHIN	*(time)*	**innerhalb einer Sekunde**
		within a second

JENSEITS

| ON THE OTHER SIDE OF | *(place)* | **jenseits des Flusses** |
| | | on the other side of the river |

KRAFT

| BY VIRTUE OF | **kraft seines Amtes** |
| | by virtue of his office |

MITTELS

| BY MEANS OF | **mittels eines Zweitschlüssels** |
| | by means of a duplicate key |

STATT

| INSTEAD OF | **statt des Bürgermeisters** |
| | instead of the mayor |

(idiom)	**stattdessen** instead of this/that

UM...WILLEN

FOR... SAKE | **um ihrer Mutter willen**
for her mother's sake
um Gottes/Himmels willen!
for God's/Heaven's sake!

WÄHREND

DURING | **während unseres Aufenthaltes in Italien**
during our stay in Italy
während dieser Zeit
during this period

E WITH THE GENITIVE OR DATIVE

DANK

THANKS TO | **dank meines guten Gedächtnisses** *(gen)*
or
dank meinem guten Gedächtnis *(dat)*
thanks to my good memory

TROTZ

IN SPITE OF | **trotz strömenden Regens** *(gen)*
or
trotz strömendem Regen *(dat)*
in spite of the pouring rain

The use of the dative with trotz is generally regarded as colloquial. Note, however the following expressions, which are standard German:

trotzdem	**trotz allem/alledem**
nonetheless	in spite of everything

WEGEN

BECAUSE OF	**wegen der hohen Preise** *(gen)*
	or
	wegen den hohen Preisen *(dat)*
	because of the high prices
	wegen meines Kindes *(gen)*
	or
	wegen meinem Kind *(dat)*
	for my child's sake

Note that the use of the dative with wegen is generally regarded as colloquial.

Note the following forms with personal pronouns:

| **meinetwegen** | **seinetwegen** *etc* |
| for my sake | for his *etc* sake |

Used colloquially, meinetwegen means 'as far as I'm concerned':

meinetwegen kann er auch mitkommen
as far as I'm concerned, he can come along too

9 CONJUNCTIONS

Conjunctions link words, phrases or clauses:

> **vor** und **hinter dem Haus**
> in front of *and* behind the house

> **schön** aber **gefährlich**
> beautiful *but* dangerous

> **nimm meinen Schirm,** damit **du nicht nass wirst**
> take my umbrella *so that* you don't get wet

They fall into two categories, coordinating and subordinating.

A COORDINATING CONJUNCTIONS

1 Definition

These link two similar words or groups of words (eg nouns, pronouns, adjectives, adverbs, prepositions, phrases or clauses).

2 The principal coordinating conjunctions:

aber	denn	oder
but	because	or
und	sondern	sowie
and	but	as well as

For the use of commas with conjunctions, see pp 249-50.

3 Word order

When introducing clauses they are followed by the normal word order:

> **ich esse gern Käse,** aber **ich trinke nicht gern Milch**
> I like cheese but I don't like milk

gehen wir ins Konzert oder bleiben wir zu Hause?
shall we go to the concert, or shall we stay at home?

sie schlief nicht ein, sondern (sie) lag hellwach im Bett
she didn't go to sleep, but lay wide awake in bed

Note that sondern is only used of two incompatible ideas:

nicht schwarz, sondern weiß   **nicht klug, sonder dumm**
not black but white   not clever but stupid

4 Conjunctions consisting of two parts:

sowohl ... als auch	nicht nur ... sondern auch
both ... and	not only ... but also
entweder ... oder	weder ... noch
either ... or	neither ... nor

sowohl deine Mutter als auch ich sind dagegen
both your mother and I are against it

nicht nur das Essen, sondern auch das Bier war sehr teuer
not only the food but also the beer was very expensive

entweder er oder sie muss weg
either he or she will have to go

weder Rom noch Neapel hat ihnen gefallen
they liked neither Rome nor Naples

5 Adverbs

Some adverbs also function as coordinating conjunctions. In such cases the order of the following subject and finite verb is reversed. Among the most common of these adverbs are:

also	außerdem	deshalb
so, therefore	in any case	therefore
inzwischen	sonst	trotzdem
meanwhile	otherwise	despite that

ich stehe morgen früh auf, ich muss also jetzt gehen
ich stehe morgen früh auf, also muss ich jetzt gehen
I'm getting up early tomorrow, so I'll have to go now

er steht heute unter Stress; er wäre sonst gekommen
er steht heute unter Stress; sonst wäre er gekommen
he's under pressure today, otherwise he would have come

sie ist 35; sie benimmt sich trotzdem wie ein Kind
sie ist 35; trotzdem benimmt sie sich wie ein Kind
she's 35; despite that she behaves like a child

B SUBORDINATING CONJUNCTIONS

1 Definition

These join a subordinate clause to another clause, in particular
a main clause. The finite verb comes at the end of a subordinate
clause. (The only exception is noted in section 3b.)

2 The principal subordinating conjunctions:

dass	als	bevor/ehe
that	when	before
nachdem	seit(dem)	während
after	since	while
wenn	als ob	damit
if, when(ever)	as if	so that
da/weil	sodass	sobald
because	with the result that	as soon as
obwohl/obgleich	ohne (...) zu	um (...) zu
although	without	in order to

bitte sag ihm, dass ich große Lust dazu hätte
please tell him that I'd love to do it

die Firma ging pleite, als sie 50 war
the firm went bust when she was 50

or:

als sie 50 war, ging die Firma pleite
when she was 50 the firm went bust

wenn wir nur Zeit hätten, würden wir so viel tun
if only we had the time we'd do so much

wenn ich dir begegne, siehst du immer so traurig aus
when(ever) I see you, you always look so sad

sie ging, als ob sie blind wäre
she was walking as if she were blind

Note that sie ging, als wäre sie blind is also possible.

mein Schirm war kaputt, sodass ich bis auf die Haut nass wurde
my umbrella was broken, so I got soaked

Note the difference between sodass and damit:

steh auf, damit ich dich sehe
stand up so (that) I can see you

Note that ohne (...) zu and um (...) zu + infinitive can only be used
when the (implicit) subject is the same in each clause:

ohne ein Wort zu sagen, schlich er aus dem Haus
without saying a word, he crept out of the house

ich koche selber, um Geld zu sparen
I cook for myself to save money

3 Omission

On occasion, dass or wenn may be omitted.

a) When the subordinate clause in question comes after the main
   clause, the finite verb in it occupies its 'normal' position:

   bitte sag ihm, ich hätte große Lust dazu
   please tell him I'd love to do it

b) When the subordinate clause comes before the main clause, the finite verb in it is the first word of the sentence:

hätten wir nur Zeit, würden wir so viel tun
had we only the time, we'd do so much

Note that in all these examples the two clauses are still separated by a comma.

4 Interrogatives

Interrogatives (eg was?, welcher? and wie?) and ob function as subordinating conjunctions in indirect questions:

der Polizist fragte mich, ob ich etwas gehört hätte
the policeman asked me if I had heard anything

dann fragte er mich, was ich gehört hätte
then he asked me what I had heard

See also pp 244–45.

10 NUMBERS AND QUANTITY

A CARDINAL NUMBERS

0	null	30	dreißig
1	eins	40	vierzig
2	zwei	50	fünfzig
3	drei	60	sechzig
4	vier	70	siebzig
5	fünf	80	achtzig
6	sechs	90	neunzig
7	sieben	100	hundert
8	acht	101	hunderteins
9	neun	130	hundertdreißig
10	zehn	200	zweihundert
11	elf	257	zweihundertsiebenundfünfzig
12	zwölf		
13	dreizehn	1 000	tausend
14	vierzehn	1 001	tausend(und)eins
15	fünfzehn	1 234	tausendzweihundertvier unddreißig
16	sechzehn		
17	siebzehn	1 990	neunzehnhundertneunzig *(date)*
18	achtzehn		
19	neunzehn	2 000	zweitausend
20	zwanzig	10 000	zehntausend
21	einundzwanzig	1 000 000	eine Million
26	sechsundzwanzig	1 198 269	eine Million hundertachtund- neunzigtausendzweihundert neunundsechzig
		2 000 000	zwei Millionen
		1 000 000 000	eine Milliarde
		1 000 000 000 000	eine Billion

a) The cardinal number 1 has the form **eins**:

- in arithmetic:

  eins plus eins gleich zwei
  one plus one equals two

- in compound numbers, when it is the last item:

  zweihunderteins   *but:*   **zweihunderteinundfünfzig**
  two hundred and one   two hundred and fifty one

- after a noun:

  Zimmer eins   **Seite eins**
  room one   page one

b) When used before a noun it is declined like the indefinite article
(*see* **p 23**), but distinguished from it by being stressed in speech:

ich habe bloß einen Euro gespart!
I only saved *one* euro!

However, if preceded by the definite article it is declined like a
normal adjective (*see* **p 62**):

den einen Schein hat er schon, den anderen aber nicht
he's got one certificate already, but not the other

Note

Note the following expressions:

- time expressions:

  um ein Uhr   *but:*   **es ist eins**
  at one o'clock   it is one o'clock

- expressions combined with **zwei**:

  jeden Tag liest er ein oder zwei Zeitungen
  every day he reads one or two papers

c) When used as a pronoun, 1 is declined like dieser:

einer der Filme **eines/eins der Bücher**
one of the films one of the books

d) zwei is sometimes replaced by zwo when it might be mistaken for drei (eg on the telephone).

e) 'in twos', 'in threes' *etc* (up to 12) is translated by zu zweit, zu dritt, zu viert, zu fünft *etc*.

f) 'tens', 'twenties' *etc* as denominations of stamps, coins and notes add the ending -er but are otherwise indeclinable, except for the dative plural:

eine Zwanziger (Marke) **ein Zwanziger (Schein)**
a 20-cent stamp a 20-euro note

g) 'dozens/hundreds/thousands of' is translated by Dutzende/Hunderte/Tausende von

h) Where English uses a comma in writing thousands *etc* German uses either a full stop or a space:
1.500.000
1 500 000
1,500,000

The German for a million, a thousand million and a billion takes the plural form:
zwei Millionen Euro/Wörter
two million euros/words

B ORDINAL NUMBERS

Note that the following numbers are usually preceded by an article *etc* and are always declined.

1st	erst-
2nd	zweit-
3rd	dritt-
4th	viert-
5th	fünft-
6th	sechst-
7th	siebt-
8th	acht-
9th	neunt-
10th	zehnt-
11th	elft-
12th	zwölft-
13th	dreizehnt-
14th	vierzehnt-
15th	fünfzehnt-
16th	sechzehnt-
17th	siebzehnt-
18th	achtzehnt-
19th	neunzehnt-
20th	zwanzigst-
21st	einundzwanzigst-
30th	dreißigst-
100th	hundertst-
101st	hunderterst-
200th	zweihundertst-
1000th	tausendst-
10,000th	zehntausendst-
1,000,000th	millionst-

a) ordinal numbers agree with the noun following them in gender and case:

meine zwölfte Stelle	**kennen Sie ihren dritten Mann?**
my twelfth job	do you know her third husband?

b) when written in figures, ordinals are followed by a full stop:

Beethovens 9. Sinfonie
Beethoven's 9th symphony

heute ist der 23. Oktober
today is the 23rd of October

After the names of kings *etc* Roman numerals with punctuation, or, less commonly, the full form in words, are used:

das gehörte Karl V./Karl dem Fünften
that belonged to Charles V/Charles the Fifth

C FRACTIONS AND PROPORTIONS

1 Fractions

Fractions are formed by substituting the -te ending of ordinal numerals with -tel. They are neuter nouns, but are only inflected in the genitive singular, adding -s:

ein Drittel
a third ($^1/_3$)

vier Fünftel
four fifths (4/5)

zweieinhalb
two and a half (2½)

but note that 'half' is translated by die Hälfte (noun) or halb- (adjective or adverb):

die Hälfte der Studenten
half the students

die größere Hälfte
the larger half

eine halbe Stunde
half an hour

ein halbes Kilo Äpfel
half a kilo of apples

halb so viel
half as much

halb tot
half dead

Note the expression:

anderthalb/eineinhalb
one and a half

2 Decimals

The English decimal point is expressed as a comma in German:

zwei Komma fünf (2,5)
two point five (2.5)

3 Arithmetic

Addition:	**zwei plus/und drei gleich fünf**	$2 + 3 = 5$
Subtraction:	**sieben minus/weniger eins gleich sechs**	$7 - 1 = 6$
Multiplication:	**vier mal zwei gleich acht**	$4 \times 2 = 8$
Division:	**neun (geteilt) durch drei gleich drei**	$9 \div 3 = 3$
Square:	**zwei hoch zwei gleich vier**	$2^2 = 4$

Note that ist, sind or macht are alternatives to gleich.

 D MEASUREMENTS AND PRICES

1 Measurements

a) *Dimensions*

dieses Zimmer ist 4 Meter (4 m) lang und 3 Meter 70 (3,70 m) breit
this room is 4 metres long and 3.70 metres wide

das Loch ist 30 cm tief   **er ist 1,80m groß**
the hole is 30 cm deep   he's 1.80 metres tall

b) *Distance*

wie weit ist es von hier bis Kassel?
how far is it from here to Kassel?

bis Kassel sind es bloß 3 Kilometer
it's only 3 kilometres to Kassel

Kassel liegt 3 km von hier (entfernt)
Kassel is 3 km (away) from here

2 Prices

was kosten die Umschläge?
how much are the envelopes?

sie kosten zwei Euro zehn (€2,10)
they're 2 euros 10

diese Bananen haben mich 3 Euro gekostet!
these bananas cost me 3 euros!

75 Cent das/pro Stück
75 cents each

5 Euro das/pro Kilo
5 euros a kilo

Weinbrand zu 10 Euro die/pro Flasche
brandy at 10 euros a bottle

das macht 34 Euro neunzig (€34,90)
that makes/comes to 34 euros 90

11 EXPRESSIONS OF TIME

A THE TIME

wie spät ist es?
what's the time?

wie viel Uhr ist es?
what's the time?

wie viel Uhr haben Sie?
what time do you make it?

a) *full hours*

es ist ein Uhr/eins
it's 1 o'clock

es ist Mittag/Mitternacht
it's 12 noon/midnight

b) *half-hours* (note the difference from English)

es ist halb vier
it's half past three

es ist vier Uhr dreißig
it's half past four

es ist halb eins (nachts/nachmittags)
it's 12.30 (at night/in the afternoon)

c) *quarter-hours*

es ist Viertel nach elf/viertel zwölf *(S. Germany)*
it's 11.15

es ist Viertel vor zehn/drei viertel zehn *(S. Germany)*
it's 9.45

d) *minutes*

es ist acht Minuten nach neun
it's 9.08

es ist sechzehn Minuten vor sechs
it's 5.44

es ist fünf vor/nach halb drei
it's 2.25/2.35

es ist zwanzig vor sieben
it's 6.40

Note that Uhr is sometimes omitted, as is Minuten

e) *a.m. and p.m.*

es ist zehn Uhr vormittags
it's 10 a.m.

es ist drei Uhr nachmittags
it's 3 p.m.

Note:

es ist zwei Uhr nachts
it's 2 a.m.

es ist acht Uhr abends
it's 8 p.m.

f) The 24 hour clock is especially used in official announcements, TV and radio announcements, timetables *etc* but can also be used in ordinary speech:

unser Zug fährt um 20 Uhr
our train leaves at 8 p.m.

die Vorstellung fängt um 19.30 Uhr (spoken: neunzehn Uhr dreißig) **an**
the performance starts at 7.30 p.m.

B THE DATE

1 Names of months, days and seasons

a) *Months* (die Monate)

Januar	January
Februar	February
März	March
April	April
Mai	May
Juni	June
Juli	July
August	August
September	September
Oktober	October
November	November
Dezember	December

b) *Days of the week* (die Wochentage)

Montag	Monday
Dienstag	Tuesday
Mittwoch	Wednesday
Donnerstag	Thursday
Freitag	Friday
Samstag	Saturday
Sonnabend *(N. Germany)*	Saturday
Sonntag	Sunday

c) *Seasons* (die Jahreszeiten)

der Frühling	spring
der Sommer	summer
der Herbst	autumn
der Winter	winter

im Juni	**am Mittwoch**	**im Herbst**
in June	on Wednesday	in the autumn

2 Dates

a) Ordinal numbers are used for the dates of the month, as in
   English, but 'of' is not translated:

   der 1. (*spoken:* **erste) Mai**   **am 11.** (*spoken:* **elften) April**
   the first of May   on the 11th of April

   Note that dates on letters and cards are usually written:

   Dortmund, (den) 3.7.2008 (*read* **den dritten Siebten zweitausendacht**)

   or

   Dortmund, den 3. Juli 2008

b) 'what's the date today?' is translated as:

   der Wievielte ist heute? *or*
   den Wievielten haben wir heute?

c) With years, German either uses no preposition or the phrase im Jahr(e) + date:

wir haben uns 1964/im Jahr(e) 1964 kennengelernt
we got to know each other in 1964

d) Year dates are read as multiples of a hundred, except for years beginning with 10- and 20-:

	1100	elfhundert
	1984	neunzehnhundertvierundachtzig
but:	1066	tausendsechsundsechzig
	2001	zweitausend(und)eins

e) On wine labels years take an invariable -er ending:

1976er Piesporter Michelsberg

C IDIOMATIC EXPRESSIONS

um 6 Uhr	at 6 o'clock
um 6 Uhr herum *(colloquial)*	round about 6 o'clock
gegen 10 Uhr	about/getting on for 10 o'clock
um Mitternacht	at midnight
gegen Mittag	towards/around midday
Punkt 3 Uhr	on the stroke of three
es ist genau 3 Uhr	it's exactly 3 o'clock
es ist 5 Uhr vorbei	it's past 5 o'clock
ab 7 Uhr	from 7 o'clock on(wards)
von 9 bis 5 Uhr	from 9 to 5 o'clock
bleib bis 2 Uhr!	stay till 2 o'clock!
das muss bis 2 Uhr fertig sein	that must be ready by 2 o'clock!
kurz vor 8 Uhr	shortly before 8 o'clock
kurz nach 9 Uhr	shortly after 9 o'clock

eine Viertelstunde	a quarter of an hour
eine halbe Stunde	half an hour
eine Dreiviertelstunde	three quarters of an hour
morgens	in the morning, every morning
am Morgen	in the morning, every morning
am nächsten Morgen	(the) next morning
eines Morgens	one morning
(am) Montagmorgen	on Monday morning
montags morgens	on Monday mornings
guten Morgen!	good morning!
abends	in the evening, every evening
am Abend	in the evening, every evening
(am) Samstagabend	on Saturday evening
samstags abends	on Saturday evenings
eines Abends	one evening
jeden Abend	every evening
guten Abend!	good evening!
nachts	at night
über Nacht	overnight
Nacht für Nacht	night after night
eines Nachts	one night
gute Nacht!	good night!
heute	today
heute früh/Morgen	this morning
heute Nacht	last night/tonight
heutzutage	nowadays
gestern	yesterday
gestern Abend	yesterday evening
vorgestern	the day before yesterday
gestern vor 8 Tagen	a week ago yesterday
morgen	tomorrow
morgen früh	tomorrow morning
übermorgen	the day after tomorrow
morgen in 8 Tagen	a week tomorrow
von heute auf morgen	at very short notice

am Sonntag	on Sunday
erst am Sonntag	not till Sunday
sonntags, jeden Sonntag	on Sundays, every Sunday
täglich	every day, daily
alltäglich	everyday, mundane
in drei Tagen	in three days' time
tagsüber	during the day
letzte/nächste Woche	last/next week
vorletzte Woche	the week before last
übernächste Woche	the week after next
wöchentlich (Wochen-)	every week, weekly
während/unter der Woche	during the week
am/übers Wochenende	at/over the weekend
letzten/nächsten Monat	last/next month
monatlich (Monats-)	every month, monthly
zwei Monate lang	for two months
vor zwei Monaten	two months ago
er verdient 5 000 Euro im Monat	he earns 5,000 euros a month
Anfang/Ende März	at the beginning/end of March
letztes/nächstes Jahr	last/next year
jährlich (Jahres-)	every year, yearly
1900/im Jahr(e) 1900	in 1900
in den 60er-Jahren	in the 60s
das Schaltjahr	leap year
im 19. Jahrhundert	in the 19th century
aus dem 15. Jh.	from the 15th century
mittelalterlich	medieval
500 v.Chr. (= vor Christus)	500 BC
500 n.Chr. (= nach Christus)	500 AD
Ostern	Easter
Pfingsten	Whitsun
Weihnachten	Christmas
Silvester	New Year's Eve

er ist 18 Jahre alt	he's 18 (years old)
sie ist in den Zwanzigern	she's in her twenties
wir sind Mitte 40	we are in our mid 40s
in mittlerem Alter	middle-aged
in diesem Alter	at this/that age
das erste Mal	the first time
zum ersten Mal	for the first time
meine Uhr geht vor/nach	my watch is fast/slow
der Zug hat 5 Minuten Verspätung	the train is 5 minutes late
im Augenblick	at the moment
früher oder später	sooner or later
mit der Zeit	in (the course of) time
im Laufe der Zeit	in (the course of) time
seit einiger Zeit	for some time past
eine Zeit lang	for a while
für/auf immer	for ever
Zeit verbringen	to spend time
Zeit vergeuden	to waste time
sich (dat) Zeit für etwas (acc) nehmen	to make time for something

12 THE SENTENCE

A WORD ORDER

1 Basic word order

a) In a simple sentence the basic word order is:

subject   finite verb (+object/objects)   (+ complement)

wir essen
we're eating

wir essen unser Frühstück
we're eating our breakfast

wir essen unser Frühstück heute in der Küche
we're eating our breakfast today in the kitchen

b) If there is both a direct and an indirect object the normal order depends on whether they are nouns or pronouns

   i) two nouns (indirect, direct)

     er gab seiner Mutter das Buch
     he gave his mother the book/he gave the book to his mother

   ii) pronoun (indirect), noun (direct)

     er gab ihr das Buch
     he gave her the book

   iii) pronoun (direct), noun (indirect)

     er gab es seiner Mutter
     he gave it to his mother

   iv) two pronouns (direct, indirect)

     er gab es ihr
     he gave it to her

c) Past participles, dependent infinitives, separable prefixes and adverbial complements usually come at the end of a sentence:

sie hat ihn in Paris zum ersten Mal gesehen
she saw him for the first time in Paris

Andrea will am Samstag eine Party veranstalten
Andrea wants to organize a party on Saturday

du lenkst mich von meiner Arbeit ab
you're distracting me from my work

das Spiel geriet heute völlig außer Kontrolle
the game got completely out of control today

Note that adverbial complements, in combination, come immediately before past participles, dependent infinitives and separable prefixes:

das Spiel ist heute völlig außer Kontrolle geraten
the game got completely out of control today

d) Inversion

It is far more common in German than in English to begin a sentence with something other than the subject. Not only adverbs and adverbial phrases but also direct and indirect objects regularly function in this way. Note, though, that only one such item may occur at the beginning of a given sentence.

i) If an adverb *etc* starts a sentence the finite verb must come immediately afterwards in second place (though it need not be the second word):

leider fällt der Unterricht heute aus
unfortunately there are no lessons today

die Hälfte des Personals hat man schon entlassen
they've already dismissed half the staff

auf den müssen Sie gut aufpassen!
you must keep a good eye on him!

ii) After inversion a pronoun subject must come directly after the finite verb:

endlich gab er mir meine Notizen zurück
he finally gave me back my notes

But a noun subject may either precede or follow a pronoun object:

morgen trifft meine Frau ihn am Flughafen
morgen trifft ihn meine Frau am Flughafen
my wife's meeting him at the airport tomorrow

iii) If a main clause comes second in a sentence inversion occurs:

wenn es schneit, machen wir einen Schneemann
if it snows we'll make a snowman

"alles Gute!" sagte sie zynisch
"all the best!" she said cynically

Note that after a wenn clause, dann may be added before the inverted main verb.

2 Subordinate Clauses

After relative pronouns (der, dessen, an dem, worauf *etc*) and subordinating conjunctions (dass, warum, obwohl *etc*) the finite verb goes to the end of the clause:

das ist das Kind, dessen Eltern beide Teenager sind
that's the child whose parents are both teenagers

kennen Sie Otto, mit dem ich jahrelang in Urlaub gefahren bin?
do you know Otto, who I've been going on holiday with for years?

When two subordinate clauses follow the same conjunction, remember to put the verb at the end of *both*:

wenn er morgen kommt und die Leitung endlich repariert …
if he comes tomorrow and finally repairs the pipes …

Note

- If two infinitive forms occur together with a finite (auxiliary) verb, this latter verb comes first:

  er weiß, dass er es nicht hätte tun sollen
  he knows that he should not have done it

- If a subordinate clause is interrupted by another clause the word order is not affected:

  sie heiratet einen Mann, der, obwohl er nicht reich ist, wenigstens gut aussieht
  she's marrying a man who, although he's not rich, is at least good-looking

 B NEGATIVES

1 Main negative words

kein, keine, kein *(indef art)*	not a, no
keiner, keine, kein(e)s *(pron)*	nobody, none
keinerlei	no ... of any sort
keineswegs	by no means
nicht	not
nicht nur ... sondern auch	not only ... but also
nicht mehr	no more
nichts	nothing
nie, niemals	never
niemand	nobody
nirgends, nirgendwo	nowhere
nirgendwohin	(to) nowhere
weder ... noch	neither ... nor

2 Position of nicht

a) nicht follows the finite verb it refers to:

ich rauche nicht
I don't smoke

du darfst nicht rauchen
you're not allowed to smoke

b) If there is an object, nicht follows it:

er braucht seine Eltern nicht
he doesn't need his parents

du hörst mir nicht zu
you're not listening to me

sie hat ihrer Mutter den Brief nicht gegeben
she didn't give her mother the letter

c) nicht precedes a noun phrase or pronoun if a contrast is involved:

gib dies nicht deinem Bruder, sondern deiner Schwester
don't give this to your brother but to your sister

ich will nicht die blauen Blumen, sondern die gelben
I don't want the blue flowers, I want the yellow ones

ich will die gelben Blumen, nicht die blauen
I want the yellow flowers, not the blue ones

Note that if there is inversion, nicht can occur in more than one position:

nicht die blauen Blumen will ich, sondern die gelben
die blauen Blumen will ich nicht, sondern die gelben

3 'not a', 'not any', 'no' + noun are usually translated by kein-, ie. nicht is not normally used together with ein:

sie braucht keinen Mann
she doesn't need a husband

ich habe keine Reiseschecks
I haven't got any traveller's cheques

keine Politesse war zu sehen
there was no traffic warden in sight

The emphatic 'not a (single)' is translated by kein- einzig-:

kein einziger Baum blieb stehen
not a (single) tree was left standing

Note that nicht may occur with ein when ein means one and a contrast is involved:

sie haben uns nicht eine, sondern zwei Flaschen gebracht
they have brought us not one, but two bottles

C DIRECT AND INDIRECT QUESTIONS

1 Direct questions

There are four basic ways of forming direct questions in German:

a) *inversion of the normal word order of a statement:*

> **rauchen Sie?**   **schläft sie?**   **regnet es?**
> do you smoke?   is she asleep?   is it raining?
>
> **liebst du mich?**   **sprechen Sie Deutsch?**
> do you love me?   do you speak German?
>
> **darf ich Ihnen meinen Mann vorstellen?**
> may I introduce my husband to you?
>
> **ist es letztes Jahr ins Englische übersetzt worden?**
> was it translated into English last year?

b) *question word(s) + finite verb (+ subject) (+ complement):*

wer?	(an) wen?	wessen?	(mit *etc*) wem?
who?	(to) who(m)?	whose?	(with *etc*) whom?
wann?	warum?		was?
when?	why?		what?
was für?	welch-?		wie?
what kind of?	which?		how?
wo?	woher?		wohin?
where?	where ... from?		where ... to?

For wo + *preposition (eg* womit?) *see pp* 107–08.

wer kommt?
who's coming?

wessen Hut ist das?
whose hat is that?

mit wem spielt sie?
who is she playing with?

wann geht er?
when is he going?

was siehst du dort?
what do you see there?

wohin fahren wir?
where are we going?

welche Bluse steht mir besser?
which blouse suits me better?

wie heißt das auf Deutsch?
what's that in German?

warum kannst du nicht schlafen?
why can't you sleep?

Note that the case after was für is determined by the preceding preposition or by the following noun's grammatical function, not by the word für:

bei was für einer Firma arbeitet sie?
in what kind of firm does she work?

was für ein Mann könnte so etwas tun?
what kind of man could do such a thing?

c) *subject + finite verb (+ complement):*

With colloquial questions of this kind, expressing disbelief, the pitch of the voice is raised on the key word, which is also emphasized:

***Oma* tanzt?!**
Grandma's dancing?!

Oma *tanzt?!*
Grandma's *dancing?!*

das soll *billig* sein?!
that's supposed to be *cheap*?!

d) *subject + finite verb (+ complement) + tag:*

In English there are many question tags, e.g. 'isn't it?', 'aren't you?', 'doesn't he?', 'can't she?', 'wouldn't we?', 'mightn't they?' *etc.* By comparison there are fewer question tags in German.

i) nicht (wahr)?

nicht (wahr)? is normally used at the end of a sentence when confirmation of a statement is expected. It is often shortened to just nicht?, especially in colloquial speech. Only the full form can stand at the beginning of a sentence, though this is uncommon:

es ist furchtbar kalt heute, nicht (wahr)?
it's terribly cold today, isn't it?

nicht wahr, sie gehört in die Mannschaft?
she should be in the team, shouldn't she?

ja? is an alternative for nicht wahr? at the end of a sentence:

du kommst heute Abend, ja?
you're coming this evening, aren't you?

ii) gell?/gelt?

In Southern Germany and Austria gell? or gelt? is frequently found in colloquial speech as an alternative to the above:

Münchner Bier schmeckt gut, gell?
Munich beer tastes good, doesn't it?

iii) oder?

oder? at the end of a sentence invites confirmation or a response:

du isst doch Fleisch, oder?
you do eat meat, don't you?

letzten Sonntag haben wir nicht gespielt, oder?
we didn't play last Sunday, (or) did we?

2 Indirect questions

a) *Definition*

Indirect questions follow a verb or a clause and are introduced by an interrogative word, eg:

explain why you're angry
I asked her who she was

b) *Word order*

German word order and punctuation differs from English. The two clauses are always separated by a comma and the finite verb comes at the end of the indirect question.

i) when the 'original' sentence contains an interrogative (eg. wann? warum? was für?):

wann geben Sie Ihr nächstes Konzert?	→ **man fragt, wann Sie Ihr nächstes Konzert geben**
when are you going to give your next concert?	people are asking when you are going to give your next concert
warum gefällt es euch nicht?	→ **sagt mal, warum es euch nicht gefällt**
why don't you like it?	tell me why you don't like it
was für Kinder unterrichten Sie?	→ **er möchte wissen, was für Kinder Sie unterrichten**
what kind of children do you teach?	he wants to know what kind of children you teach

ii) when the 'original' sentence does not contain an interrogative the indirect question is introduced by **ob**:

kann er Deutsch?	→ **ich bin gespannt, ob er Deutsch kann**
can he speak German?	I'm curious to know if he can speak German
hast du gut geschlafen?	→ **sie hat mich gefragt, ob ich gut geschlafen hätte**
did you sleep well?	she asked me if I had slept well

Note that it is occasionally necessary, as in English, to change the pronouns and the tense (and mood) of the verb in the indirect question from those of the 'original' direct question. *For the correct sequence of tenses see* p 149.

D ANSWERS ('YES' AND 'NO')

1 ja and nein

a) ja means 'yes' and is equivalent to longer positive answers such as: 'yes, it is', 'yes, I will', 'yes, he has' *etc*:

gehst du schon?	**ja(, ich muss jetzt gehen)**
are you going already?	yes(, I have to go now)

> *Note*
>
> ja can be emphasized in a number of ways:
>
> • by being repeated (ja, ja!)
>
> • in combination with wohl: jawohl! (= 'yes, indeed'), especially in the armed forces

b) nein means 'no' and is equivalent to longer negative answers such as: 'no, it isn't', 'no, I didn't' *etc*:

war es interessant?	**nein(, es war langweilig)**
was it interesting?	no(, it was boring)

Note that nein and ja used with glauben/denken translate '(don't) think so':

regnet es?	**ich glaube nein/ich glaube ja**
is it raining?	I don't think so/I think so

2 ja or doch?

ja and doch both mean 'yes', but ja is used to answer an affirmative question, and doch to contradict a negative question:

ist dieser Platz frei?	→	**ja**
is this seat taken?		yes(, it is)
liebst du mich nicht mehr?	→	**doch**
don't you love me any more?		yes(, I do)

13 TRANSLATION PROBLEMS

A GENERAL TRANSLATION PROBLEMS

1 English words not translated in German and vice versa

a) articles

   i) The indefinite article is often left out in German where it is present in English (*see* **p 22**):

   er ist leider Popsänger geworden
   unfortunately he's become a pop singer

   ii) The definite article is often used where it is omitted in English, especially with abstract nouns (*see* **p 17**):

   ich verstehe nichts von der Gärtnerei
   I know nothing about gardening

b) dass and the relative pronoun (*see* **p 220** *and* **pp 103-07**)

   These are often omitted in English but must be kept in German:

   er bestand darauf, dass ich komme
   he insisted I come

   das Getränk, das ich am liebsten mag
   the drink I like best

   Except for the dass introducing indirect statements, which is optional (*see* **p 220**):

   er behauptete, dass er krank wäre
   er behauptete, er wäre krank
   he claimed he was ill

c) After modal verbs a verb expressing motion is very often
   omitted if there is an adverb or phrase indicating direction
   (*see* p 161):

   ich muss nach Hause
   I have to go home

   willst du mit ins Kino?
   do you want to come to the cinema?

d) 'can' is sometimes omitted with verbs of perception where it is
   present in English:

   hörst du mich?
   can you hear me?

   ich spüre nichts
   I can't feel anything

e) German has many adverbs which intensify the meaning of the
   sentence as a whole. Very often there is no direct, word for
   word equivalent in English. Common examples are ja, aber, doch,
   schon, wohl:

   du hast es ja gefunden!
   you've found it!

   das ist aber gescheit!
   that is clever

   das wäre wohl besser
   that would be better

   du verstehst schon?
   you do understand?

2 Other differences

a) es

   i) es is used as an object with verbs where English has 'so'
      (*see* p 90):

      du hast es gesagt!
      you said so

      sie hat es getan
      she did so

   ii) es is used with sein to refer back to a previous word or clause
       where there is no equivalent in English:

       sie soll ehrlich sein und sie ist es auch
       she's said to be honest and she is

   iii) Note the different word order from English:

        ich bin es
        it's me

Note that 'it' must be translated by er, sie or es depending on the gender of the noun it refers to:

die Wurst stinkt; willst du sie wirklich essen?
this sausage smells; do you really want to eat it?

b) *'my', 'you' etc*

The English possessive article (my *etc*) is often translated by the definite article with parts of the body and clothes (*see* p 19):

wasch dir die Hände!   **der Hut flog ihm vom Kopf**
wash your hands   his hat flew off his head

c) *commas*

   i) In German there are no commas round an adverb within a clause:

   plötzlich fuhr er hoch
   suddenly, he jumped up

   mein Vater wollte natürlich mitspielen
   my father, of course, wanted to join in

   ii) A comma is not required:

      - when there is a common subject, conjunction or verb which is not repeated:

      er fiel und verstauchte sich den Fuß
      he fell and twisted his ankle

      weil er schneller laufen und also wahrscheinlich gewinnen kann
      because he can run more quickly and can therefore probably win

      - before und, aber, oder when the same subject is repeated:

      ich werde ihn sehen und ich werde es ihm sagen
      I will see him and I will tell him

   iii) The comma can be omitted when a coordinating conjunction which does not imply a contrast follows a main clause. Thus, main clauses linked by *und* and *oder* no longer need to be preceded by a comma, but can be if this makes the sense clearer:

Hanna leist ein Buch und Robert spielt Flöte
Hanna is reading a book and Robert is playing the flute

er traf sich mit meiner Schwester(,) und deren Freundin war auch mitgekommen
he met my sister and her friend came along too

The coordinating conjunctions affected by this are: und, oder, beziehungsweise, wie, sowie, weder ... noch, sowohl ... als (auch), entweder ... oder, nicht ... noch.

iv) Commas are still required when a contrasting coordinating conjunction separates main clauses:

der Stuhl ist alt, aber er ist bequem
the chair is old but it is comfortable

Contrasting coordinating conjunctions include: aber, doch, jedoch and sondern.

v) Coordinating conjunctions are still preceded by commas when following a subordinate clause:

er sagte, dass er morgen komme, und fuhr weg
the said that he would come tomorrow and drove off

vi) Although it is no longer necessary to insert a comma before an infinitival or participial clause, these commas can be retained, particularly when there is a need to stress a separation within the phrase or to avoid confusion:

sie hatte geplant ins Kino zu gehen
she had planned to go to the cinema

sie bot mir(,) ohne einen Augenblick zu zögern(,) ihre Hilfe an
she offered to help me without a moment's hesitation

Compare:

ich rate, ihm zu helfen
I advise that you help him

and:

ich rate ihm, zu helfen
I advise him to help

d) *agreement of subject and verb*

In English, words which are singular in form can have a plural
meaning and can be used with either a singular or a plural verb:
'the government thinks/think, the team has/have' *etc.* In German
the verb must be singular:

die Regierung beabsichtigt   **die Mannschaft hat gewonnen**
the government intend(s)   the team has (have) won

e) *direct speech*

There are various ways of punctuating direct speech in German:

„du hast recht", sagte sie
"you're right" she said

or

„du hast recht" sagte sie

or

„du hast recht", sagte sie

The last version is mostly used in print.

If 'she said' comes at the beginning then a colon is used with all
three options being available:

sie sagte: „du hast recht"
she said, "you're right"

A comma must also be used when the quoted words end in a
question mark or exclamation mark:

„was machst du da?", fragte sie
"what are you doing there?" she asked

B SPECIFIC TRANSLATION PROBLEMS

1 English verbs ending in -ing

a) As part of a continuous tense these are translated by the appropriate German tense:

he's speaking	**er spricht**
he was speaking	**er hat gesprochen/er sprach**
he had been speaking	**er hatte gesprochen**
he will be speaking	**er spricht/er wird sprechen**
he would be speaking	**er würde sprechen**

The first three often have gerade added:
er spricht gerade *etc*

b) In German the -ing form is seldom used as a predicative adjective, after the verb, as in: 'he found the film disappointing'. This usage can often be translated by the verb in its finite form:

der Film enttäuschte ihn
he found the film disappointing

c) As an adverb, the German usage is often the same as English:

"ich habe gewonnen!", sagte er lachend
"I've won", he said, laughing

d) The English -ing form used as a subject or object can often be translated by the German infinitive made into a noun:

sein Erscheinen überraschte mich
his coming surprised me

e) An infinitive with zu may also be used:

das zu sagen bringt uns nicht voran
saying that won't help

du solltest versuchen, ihn zu überzeugen
you should try convincing him

f) Very often the -ing structure has to be translated into German by a subordinate clause:

er lockte die Kunden an, indem er den Preis einiger Artikel senkte
he attracted customers by lowering the price of a few items

dadurch, dass sie uns den Raum anbot, hat sie alles ermöglicht
by offering us the room she made everything possible

g) With verbs of perception (seeing, hearing, feeling *etc*), a **wie** clause is common:

ich beobachtete, wie er sich versteckte
I saw him hiding

sie fühlte, wie das Kind sich an sie schmiegte
she felt the child snuggling up to her

h) Adverbial phrases of time with a verb in the -ing form very often become a subordinate clause in German:

bevor er hinausging, schloss er beide Türen ab
before going out, he locked both doors

als er die Fußgängerzone überquerte, traf er einen alten Freund
crossing the pedestrian precinct, he met an old friend

Similar phrases are also often translated by two main clauses joined by **und**:

er schloss beide Türen sorgfältig ab und ging hinaus
carefully closing both doors, he went out

  i) A German relative clause may also be the equivalent of an English phrase with -ing:

  die Polizei sucht eine blonde Frau, die eine grüne Tasche trägt
  the police are looking for a fair-haired woman carrying a green bag

2 'there is/are'

a) German usage often avoids direct translation, preferring one of a number of verbs:

eine Zeitung liegt auf dem Sofa
there's a newspaper on the sofa

um die Ecke steht ein Parkhaus
there's a multi-storey car park round the corner

überall herrschte Freude
there was joy everywhere

ich hätte eine Frage an dich
there's something I want to ask you

b) es gibt

es gibt is typically used in statements about the fact that something exists (or doesn't exist) in a general sense. It is followed by nouns or pronouns, both singular or plural, in the accusative case. Note also es gab, es hat(te) gegeben, es wird geben *etc*:

es gibt keine Giftschlangen in Irland
there are no poisonous snakes in Ireland

es gab damals wenig zu tun
there was little to do in those days

so was gibt es nicht mehr!
there's no such thing any more!

Note the following idiomatic uses of es gibt:

was gibt's?   **heute Abend gibt es Milchreis**
what's up?   there's rice pudding this evening

c) es ist, es sind

These are used to indicate presence, often temporary, in a defined space. es ist is followed by a singular and es sind

by a plural, both in the nominative case. With inversion es
disappears. Note also es war(en) *etc*:

es ist jemand an der Tür
there's someone at the door

es sind Würstchen im Kühlschrank
there are sausages in the fridge

Herr Ober, in meiner Suppe ist eine Fliege!
waiter, there's a fly in my soup!

in der Stadt war nicht viel los
there wasn't much happening in town

Note the expression:

es war einmal ...
once upon a time ...

3 Expressions of place

German distinguishes very precisely whether an expression of place
indicates position or motion – and if motion, then whether towards
or away from the speaker by attaching either her or hin:

POSITION	TOWARDS	AWAY FROM
wo bist du? where are you?	**woher kommst du?** where do you come from?	**wohin gehst du?** where are you going?
		sag mir, wohin du gehst tell me where you are going
bleib hier! stay here!		**geh schnell nach draußen!** go outside quickly!

sie bleibt draußen
she's staying outside

komm herein!
come in
komm hierher!
come here!

es ist dort
it's there

es kommt dorthin!
it goes there

er ist oben
he's upstairs

komm nach oben!
come upstairs!

die Kirche steht links
the church is on the left

dann gehen Sie nach links
then you go left

es ist innen schon gestrichen
it's already been painted inside

die Tür geht nach innen auf
the door opens inwards

sie warten schon drinnen
they're waiting inside

sie sitzt hinten
she's sitting at the back

er ging nach hinten
he went to the back

4 'to put'

German very often translates 'to put' by a more specific verb indicating precisely how the object is put, i.e. whether it is set down, laid down *etc*:

a) legen means the object lies:

sie legte ihre Hand auf seinen Kopf
she put her hand on his head

er legte die Zeitung auf den Stuhl
he put the newspaper on the chair

b) setzen means the object sits:

er setzte das Kind aufs Töpfchen
he put the child on the potty

Note also:

hier musst du ein Komma setzen
you have to put a comma here

c) stecken means the object goes inside something:

er steckte den Schlüssel ins Schloss
he put the key in the lock

der Spion steckte die Papiere ins Geheimfach
the spy put the papers in the secret compartment

sie steckten ihn für drei Jahre ins Gefängnis
they put him in prison for three years

d) stellen means the object stands:

er stellte die Milch in den Kühlschrank
he put the milk into the fridge

wir haben den Mahagonitisch ins Wohnzimmer gestellt
we've put the mahogany table in the living room

e) tun is the most general term for 'to put'; it is slightly colloquial:

er tat das Geld schnell in die Tasche
he quickly put the money in his pocket

tun Sie das bitte wieder weg
put it away again, please

5 'all the'

'all the' followed by a singular noun is usually translated by ganz rather than all der etc:

die ganze Mannschaft	**das ganze Geld**
all the team	all the money

6 The passive

The passive tends to be less common in German than in English. It is often replaced by man:

> **das tut man nicht**
> that isn't done

> **man behauptet, er habe das Geld gestohlen**
> he is said to have stolen the money

lassen can be used with an infinitive which has a passive sense (*see* p 145):

> **das lässt sich machen**
> that can be done

> **ich lasse das Zimmer neu tapezieren**
> I'm having the room repapered

The active form with the agent (by ...) as the subject is often used:

> **viele hielten Pele für den besten Fußballspieler der Welt**
> Pele was believed by many to be the best footballer in the world

7 'when'

a) For a single event in the future: wenn

> **wenn ich bald nach New York fliege, nehme ich dich mit**
> when I fly to New York soon I'll take you with me

> **wenn wir in Zukunft nichts zu tun haben, ruhen wir uns aus**
> in future, when we have nothing to do we're going to relax

b) For a repeated action or state in the present, past or future: wenn

> **wenn er abends Hunger hat, isst er immer Erdnüsse**
> when(ever) he's hungry in the evening he always eats peanuts

> **wenn die Sonne schien, pflegten wir im Freien zu spielen**
> whenever the sun shone we used to play out of doors

c) For a single event in the past: als

als wir euch zum ersten Mal sahen, bekamen wir einen Schock
when we saw you for the first time we got a shock

als ich sechs Jahre alt war, konnte ich noch nicht lesen
when I was six I still couldn't read

d) For questions: wann

wann war das?
when was that?

wann gehst du endlich ins Bett?
when are you eventually going to go to bed?

ich möchte wissen, wann du endlich ins Bett gehst
I'd like to know when you're eventually going to go to bed

Note that in indirect statements, wann is used following verbs of saying and many similar verbs, even if a question is not implied:

er hat mir erzählt, wann er die Entdeckung machte
he told me when he made the discovery

ich habe vergessen, wann er sie getroffen hat
I have forgotten when he met her

INDEX